Seminar Proceedings
Investment Policy

D1244482

April 18–20, 1994
Tokyo, Japan

Keith P. Ambachtsheer
Charles D. Ellis, CFA
John L. Maginn, CFA

David F. Swensen
John R. Thomas, CFA
Donald L. Tuttle, CFA, *Moderator*

Edited by Jan R. Squires, CFA

Sponsored by the

AIMR

**Association for
Investment Management
and Research**

and the

**Security Analysts
Association of Japan**

To obtain an AIMR Publications Catalog or to order additional copies of this publication, turn to page 83 or contact:

AIMR
P.O. Box 3668
Charlottesville, VA 22903
U.S.A.
Telephone: 804/980-9712
Fax: 804/980-9710

The Association for Investment Management and Research comprises the Institute of Chartered Financial Analysts and the Financial Analysts Federation.

ISBN 1-879087-42-1

Printed in the United States of America

October 1994

Table of Contents

Foreword

AIMR is pleased to publish the proceedings of the sixth annual joint SAAJ–AIMR seminar, which was held April 18–20, 1994, in Tokyo. For the second year, the proceedings have been published in both Japanese and English, allowing a wide audience of investment professionals worldwide to benefit from the seminar.

The theme of this year's seminar was investment policy—the first stage of the portfolio management process. The importance of setting investment policy has grown for institutional clients as the management of these assets has become increasingly complex and the investment environment increasingly volatile. The sessions of this seminar thus focused on how investor objectives, constraints, preferences, and market expectations translate into appropriate portfolio policies and strategies. The presentations in this proceedings discuss primarily the needs of large institutional clients—pension plans, insurance companies, and endowment funds—as they wrestle with various aspects of the vital process of establishing investment policy.

We are especially grateful to Gentaro Yura and the SAAJ Seminar Committee for their tireless efforts in organizing and managing the seminar. Thanks also go to the moderators, Mamoru Aoyama of the SAAJ and Donald L. Tuttle, CFA, of AIMR, and to all other participants in the seminar from the SAAJ—Nobumitsu Kagami, Norikazu Minoshima, Toshio Kasahara, Akira Suzuki, Tsutomu Tsuchihashi, and Shoji Yamada.

We would like to thank the speakers who contributed to the seminar and proceedings: Keith P. Ambachtsheer, K.P.A. Advisory Services, Ltd.; Charles D. Ellis, CFA, Greenwich Associates; John L. Maginn, CFA, Mutual of Omaha Insurance Company; David F. Swensen, Yale University Investments Office; and John R. Thomas, CFA, J.P. Morgan Trust Bank, Ltd. Special thanks go to Keith Ambachtsheer, Don Tuttle, and Richard D. Crawford, president of New Vision Financial, for their contributions to the case and analysis.

Finally, we also offer our gratitude to Jan R. Squires, CFA, for his outstanding editing of this publication and insightful overview.

We hope you find this book valuable as you investigate or rethink the pivotal role appropriate investment policy plays in investment management.

Katrina F. Sherrerd, CFA
Senior Vice President
Education

Biographies of Speakers

Keith P. Ambachtsheer is president of K.P.A. Advisory Services, Ltd., which he founded in 1984. He has previously served as an investment analyst with Sun Life Assurance Company, as a partner and research director of Canavost House, and as a partner and senior consultant with Pension Finance Associates. Mr. Ambachtsheer is publisher of *The Ambachtsheer Letter,* consulting editor of *Canadian Investment Review,* and a member of the editorial board of the *Financial Analysts Journal.* He is a three-time winner of the *FAJ's* Graham and Dodd Award. Mr. Ambachtsheer received a B.A. in economics and finance from the Royal Military College of Canada, earned an M.A. from the University of Western Ontario, and carried out additional graduate work at McGill University.

Charles D. Ellis, CFA, is managing partner of Greenwich Associates. He is a past chair and a member of the Executive Committee of AIMR's Board of Governors, a trustee and past chair of the Institute of Chartered Financial Analysts, a member of AIMR's Council on Education and Research, and a past member of AIMR's Education Steering Committee. Mr. Ellis has served as a member of the *Financial Analysts Journal* editorial board for 25 years. He has also written or edited numerous books and articles, one of which won a Graham and Dodd Award. Mr. Ellis holds a B.A. from Yale University, an M.B.A. from Harvard Business School, and a Ph.D. from New York University.

John L. Maginn, CFA, is senior executive vice president, chief investment officer, and treasurer of Mutual of Omaha Insurance Company and president of Mutual Asset Management Company.

He is currently chair of AIMR and has served as vice chair of the Financial Analysts Federation, as chair of AIMR's Advocacy Steering Committee, and as a member of the editorial board of *The CFA Digest.* He is a past chair of the Institute of Chartered Financial Analysts and a past president of the Omaha–Lincoln Society of Financial Analysts. Mr. Maginn received his bachelor's degree from Creighton University and an M.S. degree in finance from the University of Minnesota.

David F. Swensen is chief investment officer of Yale University's Investments Office. Prior to joining Yale in 1985, he served as senior vice president responsible for the firm's swap activities at Lehman Brothers and as an associate in corporate finance at Salomon Brothers. Mr. Swensen is a member of the Advisory Committee to the New York Stock Exchange and of the Howard Hughes Medical Institute Investment Advisory Committee. After receiving his B.A. and B.S. degrees from the University of Wisconsin at River Falls, Mr. Swensen earned a Ph.D. in economics at Yale.

John R. Thomas, CFA, is president and CEO of J.P. Morgan Trust Bank, Ltd. He joined J.P. Morgan's Investment Research Department in 1964 as a security analyst. Subsequently, he initiated a group within the department to adapt financial theory and investment technology to J.P. Morgan's investment process, to manage client portfolios, and to develop sophisticated systems for setting asset and liability policies. He has been responsible for J.P. Morgan Investment Management marketing and relationship management and was named a managing director in 1984 and a member of the firm's board of directors and Executive Committee in

1988. Mr. Thomas earned a B.A. from Ohio Wesleyan University and an M.B.A. from the Wharton School of the University of Pennsylvania.

Donald L. Tuttle, CFA, is senior vice president of the Association for Investment Management and Research, where he is responsible for CFA curriculum and examinations; formerly, he was in charge of educational programs for AIMR members. Mr. Tuttle has taught at Indiana University, where he chaired the Finance Department from 1970 to 1980, at the University of North Carolina, at the European Institute of Business Administration, at the University of Florida, at Georgetown University, and at the University of Virginia. He is also the author of numerous books and articles in leading finance journals on security analysis and portfolio management. He received his B.S., B.A., and M.B.A. degrees from the University of Florida and his Ph.D. degree from the University of North Carolina at Chapel Hill.

Investment Policy: An Overview

Jan R. Squires, CFA
Professor of Finance and General Business
Southwest Missouri State University

Change in the investment industry, which was already proceeding at a steady pace, has accelerated at a seeming breakneck speed during the past decade. The quickening of evolutionary processes in the industry has been fueled by many phenomena, two of the most notable being the development of portfolio management as a systematic process and the virtual elimination of national and market boundaries in day-to-day investment activities. The reality of these seminal developments are now almost universally recognized and accepted, but their effects and implications are still being studied and assimilated.

A vital ingredient in the portfolio management process is the establishment of investment policy. That the elements of investment policy (risk and return objectives plus various constraints) are so familiar to us as to be taken for granted is testament to the influence that *Managing Investment Portfolios*, the textbook that formalized the portfolio management process for the first time, has had in the 15 years since its first publication.[1] What may not be so clear is how investment policy making does or should reflect the now nearly total globalization of investment activities. Given that the investment policy statement combines with capital market expectations to drive the asset allocation decision, two particularly important results of this globalization have been a dramatic increase in the number, breadth, and sophistication of available asset classes and the concurrent increase in the number and size of relevant capi-

tal markets. The interface and reciprocal influences between the United States and Japanese markets are of particular interest because of the size and dominance of those two markets and the possibility that their evolution may augur the shape of other markets that are now in the early stages of development.

This proceedings, the product of a seminar jointly sponsored by AIMR and the Security Analysts Association of Japan, offers a fresh look from several institutional and cross-border perspectives at the investment policy process. Although the presentations address such diverse topics as the applicability of total quality management, the importance of clear client–manager communications, and the funding status of Japanese pension funds, a singular common theme is that the importance of articulating and implementing thoughtful investment policy cannot be overstated. That process enables both clients and managers to keep their focus in an increasingly complex global setting where rapid change seems to be the only constant.

Policy and Challenges

If investment policy is to be clearly set and closely followed, investment managers and their clients need to communicate certain information and understanding to each other. Charles Ellis discusses this need in terms of the client's agenda, the challenges facing investment professionals, and the important factors in setting and implementing investment policy.

Ellis suggests that, in meetings with investment managers, clients can ask a series of questions that will focus on the agenda of great long-term interest to the clients themselves rather than on the

---

[1] See John L. Maginn and Donald L. Tuttle (eds.), *Managing Investment Portfolios: A Dynamic Process, 1985–1986 Update* (Boston, Mass.: Warren, Gorham & Lamont, 1985).

agenda that may be of current interest to the investment managers. The questions are: How do you conceive of and make productive use of time? How do you use risk and riskiness productively? How do you conceive of and use inflation in managing investments? How do you define investment opportunity?

The challenges facing investment professionals are categorized by Ellis as artificial, unreal, or real. Artificial challenges are those, such as government regulation, that do not arise from client needs, manager capabilities, or market forces. Unreal challenges are those that cannot be met successfully in the long run, such as timing the market or beating the market rate of return. Real challenges, in contrast, are those with substantive long-term implications for clients, such as knowing the goals of specific funds and knowing the characteristics of specific investments. The process of setting long-term investment guidelines must recognize specific fund situations and depends on clear communications between client and manager.

With respect to policy implementation, Ellis points out some dangers in traditional performance measurement and emphasizes the specific responsibilities of the investment manager in carrying out policy mandates. He concludes with a challenge to investment professionals to understand themselves, the activity of investing, and the lessons of history.

Policies and Practices of North American Institutional Investors

To set the stage for a discussion of similarities and differences in the setting and implementing of investment policy in Japan and the United States, three authors address the major concerns of large North American institutional investors—insurance companies, endowment plans, and pension funds.

Life Insurance Companies

Economic, sociological, and regulatory changes have fueled a revolution in the management of insurance companies' investment portfolios. John Maginn discusses how the changes have affected the investment policies and practices of U.S. life insurance companies and compares the life companies' policies and practices with those of U.S. property and casualty (P&C) companies.

Three trends have shaped the current investment policies and practices of U.S. life insurance companies: shortened liabilities brought on by the general economic turbulence of the 1970s and 1980s, the proliferation of two-income families, and an increase in the industry's tax burden and regulatory constraints. As a result, the companies' policies and practices, although they may be strikingly different from one company to another, are all now primarily liability driven and are shaped by the types of products sold by a company, its level of competition, and the degree of regulatory and rating agency scrutiny under which it operates.

Maginn highlights dramatic and continuing changes in return requirements and specified risk tolerances. The focus of return requirements is on earning a competitive return on the assets used to fund liabilities by using such approaches as spread management and management of total return. Risk management objectives involve achieving controllable and acceptable levels of credit, interest rate, and currency risks. Maginn describes a core/satellite approach that is often used to bring return and risk objectives into sharp focus.

The investment policies of U.S. life insurance companies are constrained by limits on the scope of their investments; particularly important are liquidity, regulatory, and tax constraints. Attempting to deal with these constraints while achieving risk and return objectives has contributed to a dramatic change in the asset mix chosen by the industry; many U.S. life insurance companies are using such nontraditional asset classes as foreign bonds and derivative securities.

Maginn concludes by outlining key differences between the U.S. life and the P&C companies with respect to objectives, constraints, and asset mixes. Both segments, however, are experiencing major changes, and Maginn believes that the insurance industry will develop some of the most clearly defined investment policies among all institutional investors.

Endowment Management

The range of objectives for endowment funds is broad, and investment policy for such funds must resolve the tension between the needs for immediate income and for a growing stream of future income. David Swensen first defines the purposes of an endowment fund. He then discusses establishing the fund's investment goals, articulating its investment philosophy, and constructing a portfolio consistent with the goals and philosophy. His description of the endowment management process at Yale University is a valuable illustration of the process.

Endowments exist to help the affiliated institutions maintain operating independence, to provide operational stability, and to allow a margin of excellence in operations. To achieve these purposes, endowment management must pursue two contradictory objectives: preserving the purchasing power of assets through time and providing a substantial, stable flow of current income to the operating budget. Swensen argues that this contradiction must be reflected in the endowment's long-term spending policy and must be addressed explicitly by means of an equity bias in the endowment's investment philosophy.

Swensen illustrates in detail how portfolio construction must reflect the relative importance of the expected return contribution of asset allocation, market timing, and security selection; in his view, only asset allocation makes a sustained and positive contribution to total return. Swensen also argues that passive management is appropriate in highly efficient markets, such as that for U.S. Treasury bonds, but that active management is essential in inefficient markets, such as the venture-capital arena.

In the investment management process for the endowment fund of Yale University, U.S. equity is the core asset class

for return. Non-U.S. and private equity are added to the portfolio to enhance return, while significant holdings of long-term U.S. bonds and real estate serve as diversifying assets.

Swensen notes that the primary elements of the Yale endowment management process are the annual policy review and clear demarcation of the three types of investment decisions—policy, strategic, and tactical. He suggests that such a process can assist any manager of institutional assets in developing rational portfolios.

Pension Plans

Pension plan investment policy and implementation should reflect not only a plan's objectives, constraints, preferences, and market expectations but also the latest thinking about successful management processes and organization. Keith Ambachtsheer discusses types of pension plan arrangements in North America, important pension fund management decisions, and how the quality-management paradigm can be useful in making those management decisions.

Ambachtsheer contrasts the history, growth, and characteristics of defined-benefit and defined-contribution pension plans. The latter arrangement has been growing rapidly since the mid-1980s, particularly in the private sector and for medium-size and small employers, but defined-benefit plan assets still total nearly three times those of defined-contribution plans.

The quality-management concept has moved beyond application in the industrial sector to several service sectors. Ambachtsheer provides an interesting description of its applicability in the financial services industry. Of particular utility to pension fund managers, he contends, is the discipline imparted in addressing four basic questions: Who are the customers? What do they want? How is the product or service delivered? What is the best path to continuous improvement? The third question raises particularly important issues with respect to investment policy, fiduciary responsibilities, cost-effectiveness, and performance measurement.

Ambachtsheer concludes that investment policies in the North American pension fund industry are being determined by managers struggling with the trade-off between immunizing pension assets and increasing long-term returns to reduce funding costs. The emphasis in policy implementation is on the identification, measurement, and monitoring of cost-effectiveness in portfolio management processes.

U.S. and Japanese Pension Policies

John Thomas addresses the issue of whether the U.S. approach to setting pension fund investment policy applies in Japan. He summarizes the U.S. approach, examines the nature of Japanese capital markets and the opportunity set available to Japanese pension plans, and provides a look at the financial status of Japanese pension plans.

Interest in capital market theory and the passage of the Employee Retirement Income Security Act of 1974 have been major forces for increased diversification of U.S. pension plan assets, including investment in a wide variety of specialized asset classes and the employment of investment managers with a variety of skills and styles. U.S. corporations now consider their pension plans to be liabilities like any other financial liability; accordingly, asserts Thomas, investment policy should reflect the best way to finance the economic liability.

The U.S approach may be helpful for Japanese policymakers if Japanese capital markets function in ways similar to those of U.S. markets, especially with respect to asset pricing. Thomas provides detailed evidence to suggest that the U.S. and Japanese capital markets price assets in reasonably similar ways. Ranking asset classes by risk is similar in both markets, the distributions of returns for asset classes are comparable, and correlations among asset classes, although lower in Japan, are similar. Thomas also examines the risk–return opportunity set currently available to

Japanese pension plans, exploring the efficient frontiers generated under a variety of constrained and unconstrained scenarios.

Thomas concludes his discussion of pension policy by comparing the current funding status of U.S. and Japanese plans. He argues that Japanese pension plans are apparently underfunded on an economic basis and that fiduciary responsibility would dictate intensive examination of the financial status of each Japanese pension fund.

A Tale of Two Pension Funds

This proceedings concludes with a case study that deals with two defined-benefit pension funds, one for a public corporation and the other for a large state retirement system. The chief investment officers of each fund are preparing for formal presentations to their boards of directors regarding potential changes in strategic asset allocations. These two principals discuss in detail the evolution in investing of pension fund assets, characteristics of each of their plans, and their capital market and political expectations for the balance of the 1990s. They must analyze four different asset allocation strategies for each of three economic scenarios. Extensions of the case call for the investment officers to evaluate the effects of adding new asset classes.

Throughout the case, readers may compare these managers' situations with those of Japanese pension plan managers and consider which asset-mix strategies might be feasible for Japanese pension plans. The case analysis provides detailed discussion of the alternative strategies and suggests appropriate courses of action based on the two funds' objectives and constraints.

The case and analysis illustrate vividly how investment policy should—in fact, must—combine with capital market expectations if an appropriate asset allocation strategy is to be formulated. More importantly, they reaffirm the critical importance of the policy-making process and the resulting investment policy. All of the capital market data set forth in the case, no matter how accurate or timely, have little value if taken out of the context of setting investment policy. Similarly, the potential strategies outlined, regardless of their sophistication or detail, are impossible to evaluate without the guidance of investment policy. Thus, the two investment officers in the case, and investment professionals everywhere in our rapidly changing and borderless investment environment, are reminded that investment policy is at the heart of any portfolio management process that purports to serve the undivided interest of its clients.

Investing Policy and Challenges

Charles D. Ellis, CFA
Managing Partner
Greenwich Associates

Communication between investment managers and their clients is vital to setting and implementing sound investment policies. The quality of communication is enhanced by a focus on the client's agenda and an identification of the real challenges facing investment professionals.

Investment managers and their clients need to communicate certain information and understanding to each other if investment policy is to be clearly set and closely followed. This presentation begins with the client's agenda, proceeds to the unreal and real challenges facing investment professionals, and concludes with an outline of the important factors in setting and implementing investment policy.

The Client's Agenda

In meetings with investment managers, clients can ask a series of questions that will focus on the agenda of great long-term interest to the clients themselves rather than on the agenda that may be of current interest to the investment managers. The significant questions from the clients' perspective involve time, risk, inflation, and long-range investment opportunities.

Time

Clients should ask the investment manager, "How do you conceive of and make productive use of time?" Time is the single most important force in investing and the greatest power for good or for ill. A manager who understands time's power will be able to respond wisely and usefully to this question. Many investment managers, however, will not understand why such a question about time is being asked.

In the United States, the principal problem in investing is the manager's inability to use time productively and constructively. Most investment managers spend their days striving diligently to know what is happening at the moment in a fascinating but bewildering series of transactions involving many different instruments and markets. The compelling interest of today, this hour, this minute keeps their attention so focused on the immediate present that they have difficulty reaching out to the longer horizons that make up "real" investment time for individual investors. In investment management, the short term tends to dominate the long term—the immediate and insistent dominate the significant and enduring—because data, communications from others, and managers' own thoughts and emotions are concentrated on the short term.

Even executives responsible for pension plans or other long-term funds, who should be thinking in terms of 40 years or 50 years because that is how long the funds will remain invested, have difficulty thinking beyond five years or ten years. People who are in their 30s or 40s today are likely to live into their 80s. Their relevant investment time period is far longer than an hour or a day or a week.

The long term is where true investment value will ultimately develop or not develop. Particularly for pension funds and other institutional funds, the long term defines the central purpose of professional investment work.

Risk and Riskiness

The second question to ask an investment manager is, "How do you use risk and riskiness productively; how do you make them work for you?" Over the long term, higher rates of return are usually associated with increased riskiness—that is, higher rates of *perceived* risk, or price variability. Tversky and Kahneman have clarified the elements of risk perception by studying the behavior of human beings with regard to taking risk.[1] One question in their study asked individuals, "Will you take this bet: If you toss a coin and it comes down heads, you win ¥150; if it comes down tails, you lose ¥100?" Most people are uncomfortable taking this bet, but many will. The takers rightly estimate that it is a good bet for those sums of money. If the terms are winning ¥150,000 versus losing ¥100,000, however, almost no one will take the bet. Even if they know they can take that same bet a thousand times in succession and, within the normal distribution of odds and payouts, will thus stand to make money, almost every individual says, "No, I will not do that." The fear of loss is too important to most people, including investment managers, to take that risk. We say we will take risks, but as human beings, we are afraid of risk and will avoid it even when we would profit by taking the risk.

The second powerful phenomenon Tversky and Kahneman found was the fear of regret, or shame. Fear of having to express regret or to apologize is a powerful restraining influence on the

[1]Amos Tversky and Daniel Kahneman, "Rational Choice and the Framing of Decisions," *Journal of Business*, vol. 59, no. 4, part 2 (1986):S251–78.

way most professional investment managers do their work. We do not want to be in the position of apologizing, so we avoid risk. We avoid it too much.

The third discovery of Tversky and Kahneman was an extraordinary capacity for human beings, including investment managers, to exaggerate the importance of very unusual events with remote possibilities of occurrence. The researchers presented a large number of people the following choice: an opportunity to bet ¥300,000 and be a winner in 2 percent of the cases or an opportunity to bet ¥600,000 and be a winner in 1 percent of the cases. The choices are equal. The amount of winnings, after deducting the probability, is exactly the same; technically, the first choice is "worth" ¥6,000 and so is the second. In the first case, the bettor has a 2 percent chance of winning (2 times out of 100, the bettor will win) and the payoff is ¥300,000. In the second case, the bettor has a 1 percent chance of winning ¥600,000. The important point is that a win is very unlikely in either case. Nevertheless, the study found, people prefer the first choice, apparently because the smaller payoff and proportionately larger probability seem less extreme than the alternative choice.

A fourth phenomenon, overreaction to recent information, is clearly true for investment managers. Investment managers know yesterday's events in such detail, have so much information about these events, and are so impressed with the speed with which the information was provided, that current information overwhelms other information. Managers are hard-pressed to remember what happened a year ago. How about 10, 20, or 30 years ago? We remember a lot about what happened yesterday, a little less about what happened last week, and a good deal less about what happened a month ago; recollection of a year ago is dim and a decade ago is very dim.

The reality is that we are working with investments that will be part of the portfolio a day from now, a month from now, a year from now, even ten years from now. As the future unfolds, those investments will have been made a day ago, a month ago, a year ago, and so on. The investments may not be in the same securities, but they will be invested in essentially the same portfolios and will be the investment manager's responsibility. What we invest in today and what we will hold in the future are connected, so we should assess risk from a long-term, multiperiod perspective. We should protect our assessments from short-term domination and short-term concerns about uncertainty and from our human tendency to strive to avoid risk, and we should embrace and exploit risk in long-term, well-diversified portfolios.

Inflation

A third question investors should ask investment managers is, "How do you conceive of and use inflation in managing investments?" The simple Rule of 72—the number of years times the rate of compound interest that equals 72—allows managers to calculate quickly and easily the effect of inflation from the client's perspective. That is, if inflation is X percent, when will investors have exactly half as much purchasing power as today? How many years will such erosion take? Under the Rule of 72, 3 percent inflation takes 24 years (3 percent of $72 = 24$ years) to cut purchasing power in half. With 6 percent inflation, the 50 percent reduction arrives in 12 years. If 3 percent inflation can cut purchasing power in half in 24 years, it can cut it to one quarter in 48 years. In 48 years, investors who are young people at the beginning of the period will be elderly, and perhaps desperately in need of financial support. If inflation is 6 percent, the problem is far more severe: The investors will have 1/16 of their present purchasing power. Clearly, the challenge for long-term investing is to outgrow the cruel ravages of inflation.

Long-Range Investment Opportunity

The investor also wants to know, "How do you define investment opportunity, and how does the definition differ by type of investment?" Equities are

profoundly different from bonds. And long-term investments are extraordinarily different from short-term investments. In the short run, equities are the more dangerous; in the long run, the more dangerous investments are bonds.

Challenges to Investment Managers

Investment professionals deal with three types of challenges in addressing the client's agenda. One type is artificial, and a second type is unreal, but the third type is very real.

Artificial Challenges

Artificial challenges are those that do not arise from client needs, manager capabilities, or market forces. Regulation, whether direct governmental regulation or inappropriate regulation created by accounting requirements, is an artificial but severe challenge to long-term investment.

Of course, sound regulation can also play a constructive role. Regulation can defend the innocent individual against unfair exploitation by so-called experts or insiders. In this role, regulation has been positive.

In all countries, however, when regulation has attempted to give explicit instruction to honest experts rather than relying on their abilities to do their best work well, regulatory effectiveness has been poor. One of the problems is that regulatory authorities can easily misunderstand the fundamental natures of risk, inflation, and investment. That misunderstanding can result in forceful rules that work great harm to the long-term purposes of individual investors. An example would be rules requiring pension funds to invest too much in debt securities and too little in equities.

The long-term policies that investment managers and clients set for various portfolios reflect great national and cultural differences. International investments are three-to-four times larger in British portfolios than in U.S. portfolios, for example, and Canadian pension funds are substantially less invested in equities than U.S. or British pension funds (even though Canadian regulations are changing to allow more equity investment). Canadian pension funds and Swiss pension funds, on the other hand, have substantially greater investments in real estate than U.S. pension funds. No real reasons underlie these differences; the same markets exist for any large investor who can invest anywhere in the world. Nevertheless, the differences persist. Investment managers should question this situation.

The largest challenge we will always face in our profession is to assure that governmental regulation is never used to control basic thinking about investing. The profession needs to play a constructive role in regulation in every nation. Professionals have a responsibility to be sure that those who have regulatory authority understand the fundamental truths about investing—particularly, investing over long periods of time. Investment professionals need to reach out to regulators and help them understand the inappropriateness of using short time periods, the importance of understanding the power of inflation, and the significance of differences among investments.

Unreal Challenges

Unreal challenges are activities that can absorb a fair amount of time and energy but are not true challenges. Unreal challenges include trying to beat the market rate of return and market timing—getting into the market before it goes up, out of the market before it goes down, and back into the market before it goes up again. One reason these activities are unreal is that, with large funds, they cannot be done consistently with success. What major investment management organization has achieved a large net gain above the market return in any major market for any reasonable time through market timing? Such activities are not only a waste of time; they also distract investment managers from work they might direct at real challenges.

Real Challenges

The real challenges to investment managers are substantial. The first is to know and understand the truly long-term goals of the particular funds under their care. How many of us can state precisely the long-term goals of the pension funds, insurance funds, or endowment funds that we manage? How many of us could comfortably write such vital information down on paper and be proud to read it aloud to our clients—or aloud to ourselves—10 or 20 years from now?

Another real challenge is to know the fundamental characteristics of each type of investment, in terms of return, risk, and investment horizon—from short to medium to long term. How many of us know the optimal mix of various types of securities for the long-term goals of each particular fund under our management?

We can easily identify the challenges in managing investments. The larger challenge is managing ourselves and the other people that are joined with us in managing the investments. Investment professionals need to be fearless at those times when they might be afraid, and they need to avoid overconfidence when things look good. They need to keep taking the long-term view, even when short-term demands command their attention, and they need to manage themselves to be totally rational at all times.

We investment professionals also need to keep in mind that some who participate in our investment decisions will be younger and less experienced than we are; some, perhaps the most influential, will be older and more powerful but may be far less experienced with investing. They may care greatly about the fund being discussed but may not be expert in investing. We, as professionals, must manage their understanding.

In managing those individuals' understanding of investments and their emotions at times of severe experiences—such as market highs or market lows or during rapid drops or rises—two factors are paramount: the setting of investment policy for the long term and the ability to adhere to investment policy in the short term. One of the great football coaches summarized his 40 years of experience by saying, "It all boils down to planning the play and playing the plan"—in other words, carefully and thoughtfully deciding what to do and then being careful and certain to do what was previously decided.

Long-Term Policy Guidelines

The process of setting long-term policy guidelines must recognize the significance of specific fund situations and the importance of clear communications between client and manager.

Specific Fund Situations

In setting long-term policies, managers and clients need to keep in mind that fund situations differ enormously—in cash flows, available funds, levels of funding, and amounts of reserve money available. Pension funds exhibit the most striking differences. Enormous differences may exist among companies in the average ages of employees, but the pension portfolios meant to provide retirement benefits for those employees may exhibit no corresponding differences. For example, a large U.S. pension fund in a stable industry with almost no growth and in which the average worker age is nearly 50 may have a portfolio asset mix essentially identical to the portfolio of a company in an industry that is growing very rapidly and that anticipates continuously hiring new people during the next 10, 20, or 30 years. The first company will soon be paying out large amounts of money in current benefits. The second company, in contrast, will be rapidly adding to its pension fund. In addition to this difference in cash flows, the people's concerns are different. The old workers and the young workers are worried about entirely different things—the old about death and illness, the young about getting married and having and educating children. That the pension funds responding to the needs of those two different groups of people should be so

similar raises questions for all investment professionals.

The United States has defined-benefit and defined-contribution funds, but the defined-contribution funds are growing more rapidly than defined-benefit funds. Companies are saying to individual employees, "You will be able to control your own destiny. You will be in control of your investment." Some employees know what to do and how to do it well, and some will be lucky and their investments will work out well. Many employees, however, will be disappointed by their investing because they are not prepared for the responsibilities of considering risk, time, and investment opportunity and combining those considerations into a long-term portfolio.

For support for this prediction, consider what individual investors have thus far done with their self-directed investments. They have put their retirement monies into savings plans rather than investment plans. Most of the monies are invested in very short-term investments whose principal characteristic is safety. These investors have not even begun to look at the longer term.

Effective Communications

In setting long-term policy for an investment portfolio, the client and the manager need to communicate certain information to each other. The client needs to know the realistic expectations for each type of investment and each asset class, for both the short term and the long term *and* in the face of chaotic events—those amazing things that might happen and then disappear into the memory bank of time. What are the realistic expectations for risk, for variation, and what is the long-term average rate of return?

The client needs to communicate the economic objectives of the fund for the short, medium, and long term. Only the client can bring such information to the joint discussions with the manager that will result in investment policy.

Through communicating the necessary information, the manager and the client together can and should resolve investment policy. In most markets around the world, however, most of the decisive work is done by investment managers who are working alone and have none of the vital knowledge of the client. The clients come to the managers and say, "You know so much, you are so wise, you are so well informed, please tell us what we should do."

The best procedure would be for the client to lead and control the process of discovery and resolution of policy. The client must be responsible for decisions because only the client knows the most powerful determinants of investment policy in most organizations: the economic objectives of the fund and the noneconomic constraints on the fund. The rest of the factors in the decision are free information and are available in the marketplace.

Implementing the Decisions

The manager's responsibility is not for leading the processes of discovery and decision making; rather, it is for assuring the implementation of the decisions made for playing the plan.

Performance Measurement

In this regard, performance measurement as it is usually defined is of surprisingly little value. Many look upon performance measurement as a highly useful tool and spend a lot of time discussing and studying performance measurement data. In investment management, however, *useful* performance measurement in the short run is impossible. We cannot do anything measurably useful today, this week, or this month; it is almost impossible to do anything useful this year or in the next two or three years. The truly worthwhile things that can be done in performance measurement will cover a 10- or 20-year period.

Clients cannot wait that long, however; they need to make swifter decisions. Therefore, clients are faced with a dilemma: The data coming from the performance measurement tools are *precise* but not necessarily *accurate*, intense but

not necessarily useful. Moreover, the data either come too late to be used well or, if "timely," are not sufficiently reliable or accurate to be converted into useful decisions.

By measuring and reading performance reports and believing they have learned something from the process, clients may keep themselves from studying the meaning beyond the reports, the substance behind the data. The Greek philosopher Plato described individuals in a dark cave with a small light trying to understand reality by studying the shadows moving on the wall. Their situation is not unlike investing: Current prices of securities are shadows of reality being imaged on the cave walls, not the real business values. Are we looking at the shadows on the wall and getting very precise information about which shadow moves to the left, which to the right, which shadow is darkest, which is lightest, which gains in size, which one seems to get smaller, and *not* gaining an understanding of what is behind the shadows?

The misleading "precision" of performance measurement data shows up most clearly in one extraordinary characteristic of the U.S. industry, namely, a very high rate of hiring and firing of investment managers. The typical U.S. pension fund will hire one or more investment managers every other year, and performance measurement is almost always the justification given in these decisions. Although a fund will have several managers (not just one), changing one or more every two or three years is unwise and inappropriate.

Moreover, the manager terminated because of performance data typically outperforms the investment manager who is brought in. Thus, the process of changing investment managers imposes a cost on pension funds every year. Those in charge pay little mind, however, because the data clearly say, "For the *past* three years, this manager has failed, and for the *past* three years, this other manager has done very well." The decision makers might be better off if they looked behind the data, treating the data as shadows, and examined what is causing the performance to be different and learned what is temporary and likely to be reversed versus what is enduring and warrants action.

Some friends of mine in New York have an approximately $200 million fund with one of the highest rates of return of any endowed fund of similar size in the United States. Their annual investment committee meeting takes about an hour, during lunch, and focuses on a specific decision rule about managers. First, any manager who has had a very good rate of return and is doing the best she or he has ever done is fired. The committee sends a letter stating, "As you know, when you came to us as a manager, we told you that if you ever had a wonderful period where you had the highest rate of return, you would be fired. Today is the day. Congratulations on the wonderful return you have had, but you are fired."

The committee members then ask each other about managers who have had apparently poor investment performance, as measured by the conventional performance measurement services, for the past three or four years. They prepare a list of these managers and study the list to discover which managers have done their investing wisely and with disciplined commitment to their long-term professional convictions and commitments but happen to have had "poor performance" according to conventional measures of recent results. The committee sends such managers a letter: "We understand you have had disappointing apparent performance for the past year or so. Please be of good cheer because we have studied your actual investing beliefs and process, and we believe that the market has not justly rewarded your approach for the last year or so but will reward you over the longer term. We know your experience. We know you have lost clients. Today you are receiving a very substantial amount of money from us, and we trust your management. We are not making a mistake, and we are not fools. We have deliberately chosen to put our funds in your care because we believe you have great long-term capa-

bility as an investing professional. Our account comes to you now when you most want it. In candor, we advise you now that this account will be taken away from you when you least expect it—when your conventionally measured performance looks good. We always take the money away from a manager who has had outstanding apparent performance for the past few years. When you have outstanding performance, please be prepared: We will take our money back."

Every year, people ask how it can possibly manage this way, but the fund's performance over a 20-year period indicates that it has done just fine with its selection of managers by choosing those who were capable for the long term but were out of alignment with the current gods of the market. The same sort of thinking would have led U.S. long-term clients to move into stocks in the early 1970s but out of growth stocks in 1970, out of real estate in the late 1980s, and out of value stocks in 1990.

Key Roles in Implementation

When investment policies are being implemented, certain client and manager executives play key roles. They do not all have the same purposes and will not behave the same, but each has an important role. Investment professionals who understand those roles have a better chance of managing the total implementation process wisely.

First, the staff for any large fund has clear responsibilities (although those responsibilities may not always be made clear to them by their own organizations). These responsibilities are to clarify the issues, to provide clear alternatives to every decision being brought before the decision-making board or committee, and to assure that the investment managers follow the established policy of the fund in the particular portfolio that they manage and that all their actions conform to agreed upon policy and long-term plans.

The senior committee has two responsibilities: the formation of policy for the very longest term and the final decisions about hiring or terminating any manager who is unwilling or unable to follow that investment policy.

The investment manager's responsibility is to execute exactly what has been planned and is required and to advise the plan sponsor of the conformance of the portfolio with the intended policy. The investment manager may also be responsible for advising the senior people in the fund about how they might revise investment policy as the broad characters of markets change.

Closing Comments

The most important thing that we can do in investing is to understand ourselves. The second most important thing is to understand investing, particularly the extraordinary power of time. Finally, we can learn from what has gone before.

The philosopher George Santayana, when summarizing his life's learning, said, "Those who cannot remember the past are condemned to repeat it." Investment professionals have a wonderful opportunity to study and learn from history. To say that there is nothing new under the sun is not far wrong. Almost everything we can do in modern capital markets could be done 400 years ago in an exchange conducted in Amsterdam; they had calls, puts, calls on calls, and puts on puts. The range of investment freedom was wonderfully wide, and it enabled many people to lose large amounts of money.

The best and cheapest lessons are those you can learn from someone else's mistakes; you do not have to make the mistakes yourself in order to begin the learning. If you have not made it part of your own life's work to study the history of investment, begin the study now. As professionals, we have for one of our highest purposes to learn how to learn from history so that we do not need to learn the same lessons again and again at our clients' expense.

Question and Answer Session

Charles D. Ellis, CFA

Question: A fund may have different managers using many different investment styles, but it is seeking consistent successful performance over the long run in terms of investment philosophy and investment policy; for that purpose, what are the qualities or attributes required of its managers?

Ellis: You correctly emphasized consistent performance. Any organization that strives to achieve consistent performance will have a philosophy of investing that clearly defines the purpose that organization has in mind for itself.

Any one type of investment typically involves a profound understanding of the investment market, and with that understanding comes the awareness of at least one way of working in that market that will succeed in the long run. In common stock investing, for example, people tend to be either growth investors or value investors. Both must have a guiding light, some fundamental long-term understanding of the nature of the investment. This understanding, in turn, leads the investing organization to do certain things well that will either reduce a problem or increase an opportunity so that, in the long term, the manager will achieve a superior result for the client. Staying with that understanding consistently through time is much more important than the specific style of the investment—growth or value.

If you want to achieve success with a consistent idea or set of beliefs, you need to have a consistent process by which you do your work. For example, each of us and our families has a concept of "a happy family life," and each family has a process for achieving it. Most of us realize that the process is different for different families only when we marry and start to get acquainted with another process.

The situation is similar for achieving investment goals; the process and people must be in harmony with the goals, but the process may be different for a different "family." If you are going to be a successful investor in growth, you need to understand why that growth will develop and you need people who are skilled at understanding which companies do and do not have the requisite characteristics. A value investor needs individuals who are skilled at understanding the driving realities of value investing. To combine the investment vision, or long-term governing concept, with day-to-day work requires a process that is as consistent as the idea is consistently held. The process also requires individuals and groups of people who have a set of values and a way of working together that allow them to be effective in using the process to achieve the dream. They need to work always as a group of people who are deeply and consistently attracted to the work they do and to working with, and challenging, one another. Out of that trust, they move toward a common purpose in a common process. And they care deeply about developing and mastering the process they will follow to achieve the type of investing in which they believe.

The goal for the group and process is a "dynamic harmony" among the investment goals, investment process, and investment people. Then you have the opportunity to achieve consistent performance. Neither "perfect harmony" nor disharmony is desirable. If you have perfect harmony rather than dynamic harmony, you may have already completed the best work and may be on the way down. In an investment management organization, therefore, look for individuals who have different, but not profoundly different, beliefs. A group that admires differences and draws out the person with slightly different ideas, improves that person's ideas, and recognizes that they can learn together to improve their process and achieve their purpose. Be wary of an organization where the individual with a somewhat different approach is not wanted or an organization where the key people are frequently at odds with each other.

Question: How do you define professional ethics and professional morals for an investment professional?

Ellis: When discussing professional ethics, the focus, unfortunately, tends to be on things that are absolutely forbidden, must not be done, are obviously wrong, and so on. The discussions typically deal with breaking rules established by regulatory authorities, usually misbehavior but extending even to crime.

That focus does not truly deal with professional ethics. Of course, we should not do inappropriate or illegal things, but professional ethics require us to be sure that, over time, we are clearly holding ourselves to a higher level of accountability than mere legality and that we positively promote ethics. The ethical professional not only avoids doing what is wrong, a simple commitment, but also does the something extra that is right. Doing that something extra is not simple or easy; it can be expensive and frustrating, and we may never know for certain whether we did the truly right thing.

Ethics in our profession involves a commitment to raising standards of performance through teaching and helping young people achieve high professional standards, master the skills of the trade and use them always in the service of clients, and take responsibility for always keeping in mind the consequences of our work for our ultimate clients—for example, the individual beneficiaries of pension funds. We should be saying to ourselves, "I am going to think about the people I have never met, people I will never know, who have entrusted their funds to me and to my group. I want to think about what we might do that we will be glad about later. Knowing that those individuals will never come to our office and will never ask us difficult questions about what we are doing, never even ask us whether we fulfilled their hopes in the work that we did, I want to think about what we can do that we would be proud to have done if they were to ask."

The true ethical question is not "What did you do that was not wrong?" but "What did you do that was truly right?" Ethical behavior is doing something you are proud of, even if it did not serve your own private interest. That behavior is what enables us to be true professionals.

Investment Policies and Practices of U.S. Life Insurance Companies

John L. Maginn, CFA
*Senior Executive Vice President, Chief Investment Officer,
and Treasurer*
Mutual of Omaha Insurance Company

Economic, sociological, and regulatory changes are influencing the investment policies and practices of U.S. insurance companies. Investment policies reflect dramatic changes in return requirements and risk tolerances, and investment professionals must deal with an array of challenging and evolving constraints.

A revolution has taken place in the management of insurance company investment portfolios as a result of economic, sociological, and regulatory changes. This presentation will discuss how the changes have affected the investment policies and practices of U.S. life insurance companies and briefly compare the policies and practices of the life insurance companies with those of U.S. property and casualty companies.

Important Industry Trends

Three forces have played key roles in shaping the current investment policies and practices of U.S. life insurance companies. First, the inflation, high interest rates, and general turbulence of the U.S. economy during the 1970s and 1980s shortened the liabilities of most U.S. life insurance companies. As policyholders exercised their surrender options and policy loan privileges, insurance company investment managers had to abandon their traditional long-term investment objectives, which emphasized bonds and mortgage loans maturing in 20–30 years, and shorten the duration of their portfolios, or at least of those segments designed to fund interest-sensitive liabilities.

Second, two-income families have proliferated during the past two decades, and that trend appears to be well established. According to a 1990 estimate by the U.S. Department of Labor, both the husband and wife were employed on a full- or part-time basis in more than 60 percent of U.S. households. This change in income patterns reduced the need to purchase life insurance as protection against the premature death of the primary or sole wage earner in a household.

Third, for many decades, the regulation (by the states) and taxation (by the federal government) of the insurance industry in the United States was consistent and relatively benign. Since the mid-1980s, however, tax rules and, most recently, regulatory restraints have changed at a rapid rate. The results are a substantial increase in the industry's tax burden and an evolving maze of regulatory constraints that place relatively tight restrictions on the investment activities and flexibility of U.S. insurance companies.

The confluence of these changes is reflected in the investment policies and practices of U.S. insurance companies, particularly life insurance companies. Whereas 20 or 30 years ago, the investment activities of various U.S. life insurance companies were strikingly similar, today the differences in investment policies among companies are striking—a reflection primarily of differences in types of products sold and the characteristics of companies' policyholders. In other words, the current investment policies and practices of U.S. life companies are first and foremost *liability* driven and only secondarily shaped by capital market considerations.

Factors Determining Investment Policies and Practices

The changes in U.S. life insurance companies' policies and practices can be demonstrated by examining how the policies and practices are determined. Three forces play a primary role in shaping the investment policies of U.S. life companies: the types of products sold, the level of competition, and the degree of regulatory and rating-agency scrutiny.

Types of Products Sold

Products sold by U.S. life insurance companies can be classified into three basic categories:

- protection products, the traditional whole life and term insurance products;
- protection/savings products, which include universal life and the variable life insurance products that have been introduced in the United States during the past 15 years; and
- savings products, both fixed and variable annuities.

As shown in **Table 1**, the growth in savings products has completely reshaped the composition of U.S. life insurance companies' policy reserves. In

Table 1. Policy Reserves of U.S. Life Insurance Companies

Year	Life	Annuity	Other
1970	68.8%	26.6%	4.6%
1980	50.7	45.4	3.9
1990	29.1	67.3	3.6
1992	28.5	67.5	4.0

Source: American Council of Life Insurance.

1970, life insurance reserves were more than 68 percent of total reserves; by 1992, annuity reserves were nearly 68 percent of total reserves. So, a complete repositioning of protection versus savings products has occurred in the U.S. life insurance industry in two decades.

This shift in emphasis can be attributed to such socioeconomic factors as the increase in two-income families, improved pension benefits, the general level of affluence, and increasing longevity. Prior to and throughout much of the 1970s, Americans were concerned about premature death and sought protection primarily for lost income in such an event; during the past 15–20 years, the concern has shifted to a fear of outliving financial resources.

Level of Competition

The competitive landscape for U.S. life companies has been extended to include other industries and mutual funds, which offer savings-type products to the public. Interindustry competition has become a major factor as changes in bank regulations have enabled banks to offer life and annuity products. Banks have become aggressive sellers of annuity products and, in some cases, of full lines of life insurance products. In fact, the life insurance industry faces its greatest competitive pressures from outside the industry. Some observers expect that, within a few years, banks will be allowed to own life insurance companies, thereby underwriting insurance risk. The U.S. Congress is discussing redefinition of the scope of the banking industry and the removal of interstate restrictions on banks. In effect, traditional distinctions among various types of financial institutions are steadily being blurred by changes in regulation and by market factors.

Regulatory and Rating Scrutiny

A very recent and important factor shaping the investment policies of life insurance companies is the degree of scrutiny being applied by regulatory and rating agencies. In the United States, insurance companies are regulated by the insurance departments of the 50 states. Those departments are members of the National Association of Insurance Commissioners (NAIC), which is the central and coordinating governing body for the U.S. insurance industry. Because of the well-publicized problems surrounding the junk-bond investments (bonds with quality ratings B or below) of companies such as Executive Life Insurance Company, regulatory agencies have been under considerable pressure to tighten restrictions on insurance company investments to prevent company failures.

Regulations have been tightened for securities, mortgage loans, and real estate investments. The focus of regulation in the securities area was initially on junk bonds, which are usually associated with leveraged buyouts, but regulatory concerns have not been limited to junk bonds or even securities. In the late 1980s, a major U.S. life insurance company, Mutual Benefit Life Insurance Company, experienced severe and eventually debilitating financial problems as a result of an overconcentration in real estate investments at the time of the bear market in U.S. real estate. The lack of liquidity in real-estate-type investments contributed to the cash flow problems of Mutual Benefit and its eventual takeover by the New Jersey Insurance Department. In 1993, regulators and rating agencies raised concerns about the concentration of investments in mortgage-backed securities and the use of derivatives by U.S. insurance companies.

In the mid-1980s, the financial rating services, such as Moody's, Standard & Poor's, and Duff & Phelps, began rating life insurance companies and, eventually, property and casualty companies. These agencies also were embarrassed by the failures of Executive Life and Mutual Benefit. In both cases, one or more of the rating agencies had failed to adjust their ratings quickly enough to reflect fully the deterioration in the companies' abilities to pay claims and the companies' declining financial solvency. Subsequently, the rating agencies moved to the forefront of increased scrutiny of life insurance companies—especially their investment policies and practices.

Investment Objectives

The investment objectives of U.S. life insurance companies can be described in terms of return requirements and risk tolerance. As a result of the combined influence of new products, intensified competition, and increased watchdog activity, the investment policies and practices have been modified and are being more rigorously defined than in the past. Return requirements and specified risk tolerances have changed dramatically and are continuing to change.

Return Requirements

The focus of return requirements is on earning a competitive return on the assets used to fund liabilities, but several different approaches are taken to earning such competitive returns.

Spread management. Life insurance companies have long been considered spread managers, in that they manage the difference between the return earned on investments and the return credited to policy or annuity holders. Spread managers focus on the yield provided by fixed-income assets (bonds and mortgage loans) relative to the rate that must be credited to policy/annuity holders to be competitive and earn a satisfactory profit margin.

Most companies set crediting rates on either a weekly or monthly basis to reflect yields available in the market at that time. In determining the basis for crediting interest rates, U.S. life insurance companies use one of two methods. The *investment-year* method credits interest rates to policyholders on the basis of the yields on investments made within a particular calendar or fiscal year. For example, all products sold during 1993 would be credited interest based on yields on investments made during 1993. In contrast, the *portfolio* method credits interest rates on the basis of the average yield on an entire portfolio of investments, regardless of what year those investments were made.

In periods of declining interest rates, companies crediting by the portfolio method will typically have the opportunity to provide higher crediting rates to policyholders than companies using the investment-year method because of the lag effect of a multiyear average. Conversely, in periods of rising interest rates, companies crediting by the portfolio method will find their crediting rates lagging behind the companies using the investment-year approach.

Much time and attention is given to the management of spread by investment, actuarial, and marketing staffs of U.S. life insurance companies, because spread management has critical implications for the attainment of profit objectives and the maintenance of asset/liability management. The temptation to mismatch (by extending the duration of assets well beyond the duration of liabilities) to earn a wider spread increases the interest-rate-risk exposure of a life company.

Total-return management. During the 1980s, the concept of total return, which has long been well accepted in pension and endowment fund management, began to gain acceptance in the life insurance industry. Because of the bull market in bonds that existed during most of the decade and into the early 1990s, some life insurance investment managers shifted their attention to managing total return.

In that methodology, managers measure the interest earned plus the change in market value of fixed-income assets as being the return on which to base the crediting of earnings on life insurance policies or annuity products. The focus of attention is on managing the spread between the expected total return on actively managed bond portfolios and the crediting rates on companies' interest-sensitive products.

These differences in approaches and techniques used by U.S. life insurance companies to manage their investment portfolios and to credit earnings rates on their products are reflected in some of the differences in the overall portfolio yields of U.S. life insurance companies, as illustrated in **Table 2**. In periods of declining interest rates, the average yield on a total-return portfolio can be expected to decline more rapidly than the yield on a spread-managed portfolio. This phenomenon reflects the trading activity, and thus portfolio turnover, characteristic of a total-return portfolio and the desire to capture realized gains from the periodic, if not continuous, sale of bonds in the portfolio.

Return requirements for surplus. The prevailing literature on life insurance company investments is relatively scant and devotes little attention to the investment of surplus funds. Life insurance companies' return requirements do include as an objective, however, the earning of competitive returns on assets that fund surplus.

Surplus in the insurance industry is extremely important, both as an indicator of financial stability and as a basis for

Table 2. Portfolio Yields of U.S. Life Insurance Companies

Year	Industry Average Yield	Major Life Companies		
		Prudential Life	Lincoln National Life	Equitable– New York Life
1970	5.34%	5.56%	5.47%	5.32%
1980	8.06	7.85	8.09	8.18
1990	9.31	8.80	8.68	7.26
1992	8.58	8.31	8.54	7.50

Sources: A.M. Best & Co. and the American Council of Life Insurance.

expansion of the business. Thus, growth in surplus, through operations and investments, is an important measure in the industry.

When selecting investments for surplus funds, investment managers have typically sought out assets that provide the potential for capital appreciation, such as common stocks, real estate, and to a lesser extent, venture capital. Common stock returns are measured on the basis of annual total returns relative, generally, to some market index, such as the S&P 500. For real estate investments, the internal rate of return during a holding period of as much as 10–20 years is used as a measure of return potential. Similarly, for venture-capital investing, the internal rate of return, generally for an intermediate holding period of 8–10 years, is used as a return measure.

Risk Tolerance

Confidence in the ability of an insurance company to pay benefits as they come due is a crucial element in the financial foundation of the U.S. economy. Thus, insurance companies are sensitive to the risk of any significant chance of principal loss or any significant interruption of investment income. The risk-management objective of U.S. life insurance companies can be defined as achieving controllable and acceptable levels of three types of risk: credit, interest rate, and currency.

Credit risk. Life insurance companies attempt to achieve a controllable level of credit risk through internal limits on credit quality. Bonds rated Baa/BBB or better are considered to be investment grade. Some companies have no self-imposed limits on holdings that fall within the investment-grade classification; other, more conservative, companies limit the percentage of holdings, especially in Baa/BBB-rated securities. Many companies purchase bonds rated below Baa/BBB on an exception basis; that is, such investments require prior approval by an investment committee and/or must be limited in the amount invested (as a percentage of assets or absolute dollar amount) and/or

scope (the lowest credit rating permitted, for example, might be a single B).

The NAIC inaugurated a credit-risk classification system for insurance company bond holdings in 1992. The system uses six classifications of credit risk. **Table 3** shows the relationship between the NAIC classifications and the financial ratings of Moody's for various types of bonds. The table also shows the holdings of U.S. life insurance company bonds by NAIC classification at year-end 1992. The insurance industry at that time had limited exposure to non-investment-grade bonds; investment-grade bonds accounted for 92.6 percent of total bond holdings and 59.1 percent of total assets.

Table 3. Bonds Held by U.S. Life Insurance Companies by Quality Class, December 31, 1992

NAIC Class	Comparable Moody's Rating	Percent of Total Bonds	Percent of Total Assets
High quality			
1	Aaa, Aa, A	71.0%	45.3%
2	Baa	21.6	13.8
Medium quality			
3	Ba	3.1	1.9
Low quality			
4	B	2.6	1.7
5	Caa, Ca, C	1.1	0.7
6	D	0.6	0.4
Total		100.0%	63.8%

Source: A.M. Best & Co.

Interest rate risk. Given the interest-sensitive nature of the majority of modern life insurance products, interest rate risk is clearly the most pervasive of the risks being managed by life insurance company investment professionals. Financial theory points out that interest rate risk is also difficult to anticipate and largely nondiversifiable. These characteristics explain the time and attention that the U.S. life insurance industry devotes to asset/liability management.

The purpose of asset/liability management techniques is to align the interest-rate-risk characteristics of assets with those of liabilities in such a way that both sides of the insurance company's balance sheet are synchronized in relation to the effects expected from changes in interest rates. To accomplish this synchronization, a life insurance company's actuaries determine, through cash flow testing and modeling of interest rate scenarios, the expected duration of liabilities. The goal is to simulate the optionality of the interest-sensitive products being offered by the company.

One option in such products is the option to surrender a policy—typically, with penalties in the early years of a policy or annuity's life and without penalties in the later years (for example, the sixth year and beyond). Another option involves the policy loan privileges included in many traditional life insurance policies. Either of these options can be triggered by changes in interest rates, and the resulting cash flow/liquidity needs can occur at a time of declining bond prices, which forces insurance companies to sell assets at a loss. Asset/liability management attempts to mitigate this risk of forced sale.

Because of the different option features in various types of life and annuity products, most U.S. life insurance companies segment their portfolios so as to group liabilities by similar interest-rate-sensitivity characteristics. Investment managers then attempt to construct portfolios by segment so that the most appropriate and attractive assets, both by type and duration, are being used to fund the various product segments. By aligning the duration of assets and the duration of liabilities, the managers can measure, monitor, and manage degrees of interest rate risk.

Table 4 illustrates asset/liability management by way of an example of *hypothetical* duration targets, credit-risk parameters, and product segments for a U.S. life company. In panel A, various product segments are identified and examples of asset/liability durations are listed. The durations shown for liabilities are only representative in nature; differences in product offerings of various companies could result in rather broad ranges of liability durations. Panel A of Table 4

also reflects the policy of limiting interest rate risk by having relatively small differences between the target durations of liabilities and assets. Again, individual companies can have widely varying policies with regard to the allowable gap between asset and liability durations. Panel B of Table 4 is an example of how asset/liability management translates into portfolio specifications; such decisions as types of assets, ranges of maturity or average life, and credit quality are addressed for those asset classes deemed to be appropriate for funding a particular product segment (in this case, traditional whole life).

Tolerance for interest rate risk, or for the degree of duration mismatch, varies by company, but the sharp increase in U.S. interest rates starting in October 1993 focused increased attention on interest rate risk (especially in mortgage-backed and derivative securities) from regulators and rating agencies. Just as their scrutiny has led to modification and limitations on the credit risk taken by insurance companies, their scrutiny may lead to new limitations on the taking of interest rate risks.

Currency risk. The insurance regulations in most states limit life insurance company holdings of foreign securities, whether denominated in U.S. dollars or foreign currency, to 5 percent of total assets. Thus, U.S. life insurance companies have only limited opportunities to manage currency risk to achieve additional return. To moderate currency risk, most U.S. life companies that invest in foreign securities denominated in foreign currencies diversify their holdings by currency. Some also use hedging strategies to minimize further or neutralize the risk of exchange rate changes. Most studies of foreign investments indicate, however, that a significant part of the return advantage attributable to foreign securities is associated with changes in exchange rates.

Financial literature also points out the covariance benefits of using foreign securities in a portfolio to diversify interest rate and credit risks. Thus, as the trend to globalization of capital markets

Table 4. An Example of Asset/Liability Management Applied to a U.S. Life Insurance Company

A. Duration by product segment

Product Segment	Duration (in years) of	
	Assets (actual)	Liabilities (target)
Traditional whole life	5.0	5.2
Universal life	4.2	4.0
Single premium deferred annuity	3.9	3.8
Guaranteed investment contract	2.5	2.3

B. Portfolio segment specifications

Traditional Whole Life	Maturity or Average Life (years)	Quality
Corporate bonds		
Public bonds	3–12	A–Baa
Private-placement bonds	3–12	A–Baa
Mortgage-backed bonds	3–10	Aaa
Mortgage loans	3–10	—

Source: John L. Maginn.

continues, one of the results could be some expansion of the ability of U.S. life insurance companies to use foreign securities as return-enhancing and risk-diversifying assets.

Determining acceptable risk levels. As noted earlier, much regulatory and rating-agency time and attention is being given to determining the acceptable level of risk for U.S. life insurance companies. Traditionally, this attention has primarily addressed credit risk; investment laws in the United States limit the percentage of holdings by credit quality, especially for bonds rated below Baa/BBB, and by type of asset (especially mortgage loans, common stocks, and real estate). In addition, the NAIC inaugurated an asset valuation reserve (AVR) in 1992, which requires insurance companies to set aside reserves based on the risk characteristics of their assets; the AVR can be thought of as a bad-debt or credit-risk reserve.

In 1993, U.S. regulators introduced the concept of risk-based capital for U.S. life insurance companies. These regulations require that a U.S. life insurance company maintain a level of capital and surplus that is based on the risk charac-

teristics of that company's assets and liabilities. Prior to the advent of the concept of risk-based capital, most states set minimum dollar amounts of required capital and surplus regardless of the nature of the company's assets and liabilities. Risk-based capital should prove to be a much more accurate measure of risk exposure and risk tolerance than the previous approach, and additional rules related to risk-based capital will undoubtedly be developed through application and experience.

Table 5 compares the risk factors for various asset classes as specified under the risk-based capital (RBC) and AVR regulations; the difference in factors under the two types of regulation is clear. The AVR was established before the RBC requirements were defined, and regulatory agencies are attempting to synchronize the factors.

Core/Satellite Approach

To bring their investment objectives into focus, and to highlight the differences in asset groupings used to fund liabilities and to fund surplus, many life insurance companies are using a core/satellite approach for a broad definition of their in-

Table 5. Comparison of Risk Factors for RBC and AVR

Item	NAIC Category	Bonds		Unaffiliated Preferred Stock	
		RBC	AVR	RBC	AVR
Bonds and preferred					
stock	1	0.3%	1.0%	2.3%	3.0%
	2	1.0	2.0	3.0	4.0
	3	4.0	5.0	6.0	7.0
	4	9.0	10.0	11.0	12.0
	5	20.0	20.0	22.0	22.0
	6	30.0	20.0	30.0	22.0
Commercial mortgages					
In good standing				3.0	3.5
90 days overdue				6.0	3.5[a]
Real estate					
Company occupied				10.0	7.5
Investment				10.0	7.5
Foreclosed				15.0	7.5

Source: Goldman, Sachs & Co.

[a] Adjusted for percentage of nonperforming assets.

vestment policies. **Figure 1** depicts funding strategies for assets and liabilities within risk-management parameters. The large circle on the left side reflects the core investments used to fund typical life insurance liabilities. The size and position of the circle suggest that the vast majority of funding assets for liabilities would be investment-grade bonds or mortgage loans; combined, those assets would provide an appropriate level of liquidity on the basis of both maturity and cash flow. The smaller circles overlapping the top of the outer ring of the large circle depict the use of small but intensively managed portfolios of higher risk assets to enhance returns from the liability-funding portfolio. The small circles at the bottom within the dotted lines depict strategies to control risk. Common stocks and real estate are the logical core assets for funding

Figure 1. Core/Satellite Approach to Achieving Investment Objectives

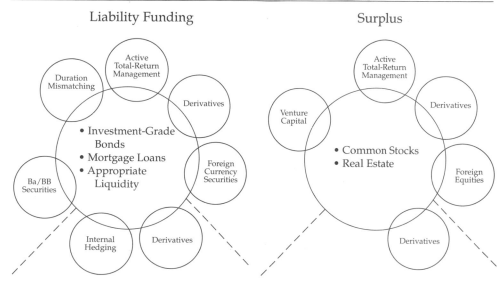

Source: Mutual of Omaha Insurance Co.

surplus, with venture capital and other higher risk assets used in smaller proportions to enhance return and derivatives to control risk.

In addition to providing insights into the process of setting investment policy, the core/satellite approach has proved to be an effective way of communicating with investment committees, boards of directors, rating agencies, and regulators.

Investment Constraints

Investment policies of U.S. life insurance companies are constrained by limits on the scope of their investments. Of particular importance are liquidity, regulatory, and tax constraints.

Liquidity

Because life insurance and annuity products are basically promises to pay upon death or at some time in the future, a key investment constraint for the insurance companies is a need for liquidity, for funding operational working capital and funding unexpected surrender levels and/or policy loans. The liquidity position of insurance companies is also of prime concern to regulators and rating agencies. Too often, U.S. life insurance companies devote inadequate attention to liquidity needs.

Historically, liabilities of the companies were relatively long term; therefore, current liquidity needs were relatively modest. The volatility in interest rates in the United States in the past two decades, however, has materially shortened the duration of the liabilities of U.S. life insurance companies and increased their liquidity needs accordingly.

Regulation

As noted earlier, regulatory factors are important constraints for U.S. life insurance companies. In addition to the recent AVR and RBC requirements, regulators are also debating a new model investment law that would define limits for holdings of certain types of assets.

The Financial Accounting Standards Board has recently (Financial Accounting Statement No. 115) required U.S. life insurance companies to mark their bond portfolios to market. This change in accounting, which is in effect as of 1994 for stock life insurance companies in the United States, is an example of a well-intentioned but unbalanced approach. Marking to market bond assets only, rather than all assets and all liabilities, will create major distortions of the surplus positions of U.S. life insurance companies. In some cases, such distortions could lead to erroneous conclusions about the financial stability of a company. Fortunately, discussions are continuing about broadening the market-value principle to apply to both sides of the balance sheet and to all, or at least most, asset classes.

Taxes

As if heightened liquidity needs and increased regulatory constraints were not enough, the U.S. life insurance industry has also shouldered a substantial tax burden through the tax on deferred acquisition costs and other changes in income tax law that have accumulated since the mid-1980s. U.S. life insurance companies today commonly have effective federal income tax rates that can reach or exceed 50 percent (as compared with the current corporate tax rate of 35 percent).

Asset-Mix Change

A reflection of the scope of the changes in the U.S. life insurance industry in the past 20 years is the change in asset mix, as shown in **Table 6**. The traditional list is types of investments favored by most companies through the mid-1970s. The contemporary list is asset classes currently used by many, although not all, U.S. life insurance companies. Clearly, recent capital market changes, particularly the financial engineering on Wall Street, have broadened the array of assets available to and being used by U.S. life insurance companies to meet their investment objectives and to deal with the constraints under which they operate.

Table 6. Changes in Life Insurance Industry's Asset Mix

Traditional	Contemporary

Bonds, domestic (Aaa–Baa)	Bonds
	  Domestic
	    Aaa–Ba quality
	    Junk bonds
	  Foreign
	    Hedged
	    Unhedged

Mortgage loans, residential	Mortgage loans, commercial and residential
Stocks, common and preferred	Common stocks, domestic and foreign
Equity real estate	Equity real estate

Other, venture capital	Venture capital
	Derivative instruments
	  Futures
	  Options
	  Interest rate swaps

U.S. Property and Casualty Companies

The investment policies and practices of U.S. property and casualty insurance companies are significantly different from those of life insurance companies because the liabilities, risk factors, and tax considerations are distinctly different. These differences are reflected in the return requirements, risk tolerances, and investment constraints of U.S. property and casualty companies.

Investment Objectives

The investment objectives of U.S. property and casualty companies are designed to fund liabilities that are materially different from the liabilities of the life insurance companies. As their name implies, property and casualty coverages are designed to reimburse for physical or monetary damages incurred. Therefore, no earnings rates are credited on typical policies, and most property and casualty liabilities are not directly interest rate sensitive. These insurers do, however, face greater uncertainty than life insurance companies and, potentially, greater frequency of claims.

Return objectives. The return requirement for typical property and casualty companies is to maximize the after-tax yield on their fixed-income investment portfolios. In addition, these companies typically have much larger common stock portfolios than do U.S. life insurance companies.

In recent years, U.S. property and casualty companies have embarked on more active management of their bond portfolios than in the past. The goal is to enhance the typical return contribution of the bond portfolio; a side benefit is the augmentation of portfolio liquidity characteristics.

Property and casualty companies use common stocks not only to fund surplus but also to fund some portion of liabilities. Common stock investments in a property and casualty company's portfolio are measured on a total-return basis, typically relative to a market index such as the S&P 500.

Risk tolerance. Management of investment risk is also a key factor for U.S. property and casualty companies. These companies attempt to identify an acceptable level of risk and demonstrate an ability to control investment risk. The liquidity requirements of property and casualty insurers limit their risk tolerances and influence their investment policies.

Investment Constraints

The exposure of property and casualty companies to unpredictable and catastrophic claims requires their investment staffs to focus on the high liquidity and marketability of portfolio assets. These liquidity needs have created a different regulatory attitude toward the property and casualty companies from the attitude toward life insurance companies. The companies' liquidity needs and this regulatory attitude are part of the reason common stocks have long been an acceptable asset holding for U.S. property and casualty companies. Whereas U.S. life insurance companies are typically limited to no more than 10 percent of assets in common stocks, property and casualty companies typically maintain percentages of 20 percent or more of their portfolios in stock.

The differences in the regulatory approaches suggest that regulators reconsider the role of common stocks in life insurance investing. The narrowing difference currently being experienced in the U.S. markets between the volatility of bond prices and that of stock prices may encourage such a reexamination.

Investment law as applied to property and casualty insurance companies is far less restrictive than as applied to life insurance companies. RBC and AVR requirements will be applied to the U.S. property and casualty industry, however, in the mid-1990s. These concepts are new for this industry and are expected to constrain the risks taken and risk exposure of the typical property and casualty company.

Although income taxes are a consideration in shaping investment policy for property and casualty insurers, their income taxes are not nearly as burdensome or restrictive as those of the life insurance companies. The effective tax rates for property and casualty companies are typically 35 percent or less.

Asset Distribution

Key differences between U.S. property and casualty and life insurance companies in asset mix and investment policies can be identified by examining their respective asset holdings. **Table 7** outlines the typical holdings of companies in both industries at year-end 1992. Significant differences exist in the holdings of common stocks and non-investment-grade

Table 7. Comparison of Asset Mixes

Admitted Assets	Property/ Casualty	Life/ Health
Cash and short-term assets	6%	3%
Stocks	11	2
Bonds (investment grade)	<u>60</u>	<u>51</u>
Total liquid assets	77	56
Bonds (not investment grade)	0	3
Mortgage loans	0	14
Real estate	0	3
Affiliated companies	4	2
Other assets	<u>19</u>	<u>22</u>
Total assets	100%	100%

Source: A.M. Best & Co.

bonds, mortgage loans, and real estate.

Conclusion

The U.S. insurance industry, particularly the life insurance segment, is experiencing major changes. Multiple factors are influencing the investment policies and practices of insurance companies. Investment professionals are being challenged to manage risk more adroitly than in the past and meet much more rigorous regulatory and rating-agency requirements. One result will be the evolution within the insurance industry of some of the most clearly defined investment policies among all institutional investors.

Question and Answer Session

John L. Maginn, CFA

Question: You suggested that life companies should increase their stock investments, but can they do so under RBC requirements, which consider the stock ratio already too high?

Maginn: We are faced with a conflict between regulation and investment theory today; the conflict poses an educational task for the industry. The hope is that actuaries and, in turn, regulators can be convinced of several factors already known to investment professionals.

First, common stocks are considered riskier assets by regulators because of the variability of their returns and the traditional volatility in stock prices. Bond prices in the United States today, however, have as much as or more volatility than stock prices. On a market-value basis, stocks are not a riskier asset. Stock investments would take advantage of financial theory's conclusion that expected returns are higher over long time periods for common stocks than for fixed-income instruments.

Second, insurance companies have very long-term liabilities. The duration of some liabilities is longer than the duration available to investors on any fixed-income investment. Asset/liability management, in trying to relate the duration of assets to the duration of liabilities, needs the latitude to invest in an asset of much longer duration than bonds, such as a common stock.

Question: Are the AVR and RBC regulations necessary for the healthy operation of insurance companies in the United States, and are these requirements likely to be tightened in the future?

Maginn: AVR, because it is similar to the bad-debt reserve for a manufacturing company with receivables, plays an important role. Initially, AVR was used in the United States only for bonds and common stocks; it was used in mortgage loans and real estate for the first time in 1992. AVR protects the policyholder and the company by acting as a buffer so that losses are not taken directly through surplus.

One problem in the United States is the difference between AVR and RBC. Table 5 illustrated that the two regulatory approaches require different percentages of reserves for the same asset types.

In addition, from a pure investment standpoint, AVR and RBC reserve requirements on common stocks are far too high in relation to the asset class's actual risk and severely constrain the insurance industry from taking full advantage of that asset class. The insurance industry in the United States needs synchronization of these regulations and recognition by the regulators that equity assets, particularly common stocks, are not nearly as risky as perceived.

Question: How do U.S. firms cope with the constraints on matching durations of assets and liabilities; for example, do they issue commercial paper to shorten the duration on the liability side while also working on the asset side to reduce the mismatch?

Maginn: Even with the breadth of investments available in the U.S. markets, finding the combination of assets to provide the desired duration characteristics from the perspective of asset/liability management is difficult. Therefore, derivatives are playing an increasing role.

Companies currently use several techniques to modify the duration characteristics of assets. Insurance companies borrow in both the commercial paper and, most recently, the surplus note markets. (Surplus notes are subordinated debentures sold by insurance companies.) Insurance companies are also using interest rate swaps, futures, and options to modify the duration of assets to achieve balance with the duration of liabilities. Currently, U.S. regulators are concerned about the use of derivatives, not only by insurance companies but also by hedge funds and pension funds. Regulators need to understand the favorable aspects of derivative securities, however—that such securities can be used to modify risk rather than to magnify it. Although derivatives can certainly be used in a speculative way, they can also be honestly used to modify risk in a hedging context. Fortunately, very useful discussions of derivatives are occurring among the regulatory agencies, including the Securities and Exchange Commission. The discussions may result in some additional rules and regulations for derivatives, but the beneficial effect for the insurance industry should be recognition of the acceptability of derivatives for hedging purposes, particularly hedging in the context of asset/liability management.

Question: When life and property companies make stock investments in Japan, they must purchase and hold some stocks for relationship purposes. The expected returns for Japanese property or life insurance companies are fixed by regulation, which may be a constraint. What is the situation in the United States regarding relationship investing, and what are other differences between the industries in Japan and the United States?

Maginn: Relationship investing is not nearly as important in the United

States as in Japan and is usually not a factor to be considered. My understanding of the Japanese common stock market and the investment practices of insurance companies is that only part of the companies' common stock investments are relationship investments; the companies have the freedom and flexibility to make general market investments.

The returns provided on insurance products in Japan have not faced the competition typically faced in the United States. Japan does have postal savings plans, however, and certain other alternatives. About five years ago, Japanese insurance companies offered premium payment plans that were expected to earn relatively high rates of return for a ten-year period. Those high rates of return allowed the policyholders to pay their premiums in about two years after the product came out. When interest rates declined, the product became very troublesome for the insurance companies.

Japanese insurance companies face the same external competition from investment management firms as those in the United States. That competition is healthy and very much to the benefit of investors and savers, but insurance company investment professionals need to learn how to manage in a competitive environment.

Currently, Japan also has the advantage of not having the volatility in interest rates being experienced in the United States. This volatility may well become a worldwide phenomenon, however. During the next few decades, the returns offered on insurance or savings products may be more closely related, even though the products may be in different countries. For example, the return available on an insurance policy in the United States and that on a policy in Japan may be more closely related than at present.

Question: When U.S. insurance companies set up investment objectives or policies, what procedures do they follow? Who is responsible for preparing such policy statements? How often do they have to be changed or revised?

Maginn: Most, but not all, insurance companies today have investment policy statements. Regulators are beginning to recognize the importance of stated investment policy, and the important role of an investment policy statement in any portfolio is emphasized by numerous academicians and practitioners.

Most investment policy statements are developed by a company's investment staff—working on its own or working with an investment committee of the board of directors. Regulation in the United States typically requires that a company's board of directors or a board-level investment committee be responsible for overseeing the investment policy (if not actually setting it) and assuring that investment policy is being followed.

A model investment regulation is being formulated in the United States. One new requirement will apparently be that investment policy be approved by the full board of directors and that the board determine, first, that the investment policy is appropriate for the insurance company and, second, that the investment staff is capable of carrying out the policy. In addition, a probable requirement will be an annual review of the investment policy by the board of directors.

Mutual of Omaha has had investment policy statements for many years, and they have always been approved annually by the investment committee. Starting in 1994, policy statements are being approved by the board of directors as well as the investment committee.

The investment committee also receives monthly reports of all transactions. In addition, I report quarterly to the board of directors on all investment transactions, both purchases and sales, and how they fit within the investment policy and regulations governing our portfolios.

Endowment Management

David F. Swensen
Chief Investment Officer
Yale University Investments Office

Endowment fund managers must resolve the tension between competing needs for immediate income and for a growing stream of future income. A well-conceived management process based on certain key principles has helped a major U.S. educational endowment formulate and implement sensible investment policies to meet competing objectives.

Using the challenges of endowment management, this presentation outlines a framework for institutional investors: defining the purposes of an investment fund, establishing the goals of investment management, articulating the investment philosophy, and constructing a portfolio that is consistent with the philosophy and that meets the established goals. Particular emphasis is placed on the basic tension between the need for immediate income and pressures for preservation of assets. The presentation closes with a description of the investment management process followed at Yale University. This process and the principles underlying endowment management can assist in formulating sensible investment policies for institutional investors in any setting.

Purposes of Endowment Funds

An endowment represents the permanent funds of a college or university, a pool of assets designed to provide revenue that will support the operations of the educational institution forever. To maintain intergenerational neutrality, the degree of the endowment's support should be the same 5, 50, or 500 years from now as it is today.

Institutions accumulate endowments to achieve several purposes. One is to help the institution maintain operating independence. An educational institution that relies on current income sources to support operations must recognize that those current flows frequently are received with strings attached. For example, when the government provides grants to support university research, those grants often come with restrictions that influence university-wide operations. Similarly, to the extent that the university relies on donor gifts for current use, those donors may have a significant impact on the university's activities. Even universities that rely heavily on tuition income from students may be constrained by that dependency. Such institutions may be forced to respond to the wishes and needs of the current student body to attract a sufficient number of students to maintain current operations.

In short, overreliance on short-term sources of income requires the institution to respond to a combination of explicit and implicit pressures. The institution with an independent source of funds, such as an endowment, has a greater chance of maintaining independence from such pressures.

A second purpose of endowment accumulation is to provide operational stability. Short-term funding sources may diminish or disappear, but a permanent fund can provide a stable flow of resources to the operating budget of the institution.

The final purpose of endowment accumulation is to allow a margin of excellence in operations. Major private U.S. research universities have roughly similar revenue streams from tuition, grants, and gifts. A significant endowment creates an incremental revenue stream that allows the better endowed institution to achieve a margin of excellence in its operations.

Goals of Endowment Management

The two significant goals of endowment management are to preserve the purchasing power of the assets throughout time and to provide a substantial, stable flow of resources to the operating budget. Preserving the purchasing power of assets allows future generations to benefit from the endowment at the same level as the current generation. Providing substantial resources to current operations supports the institution's current scholarly activities.

A direct and clear trade-off in economic terms exists between the two goals. To the extent that managers are strict about maintaining the purchasing power of endowment assets, great volatility is introduced into the flow of resources delivered to the operating budget. To the extent that managers are strict about providing a sizable and stable flow of resources to the operating budget, substantial volatility is introduced into the purchasing power of endowment assets.

This trade-off can be illustrated by considering two extreme policies that might be used to determine the annual spending from an endowment. On one hand, if the institution could spend only the real returns generated by the portfolio, asset purchasing power could be maintained perfectly. Assume investment returns are 10 percent in one year and inflation is 4 percent. If the 6 percent real return on endowment value is distributed

to the operating units and the 4 percent attributable to inflation is reinvested in the endowment fund to maintain purchasing power, all constituents are satisfied. In the following year, assume that investment returns are only 2 percent and inflation is 7 percent. Now the institution faces a serious problem. Compensation for inflation requires a 7 percent reinvestment in the endowment, but the fund only generated a return of 2 percent. The endowment manager cannot go to the operating units and ask for 5 percent rebates to maintain the purchasing power of assets. Thus, a policy that seeks to maintain asset purchasing power without exception is not feasible.

The other policy extreme, pursuing the goal of providing a completely stable flow of resources to the operating budget, could be accomplished by spending a fixed amount that is increased each year by the amount of inflation. In the short term, the flow of resources from the endowment to the operating budget will be perfectly stable and quite predictable. Under normal market conditions, such a policy might not be harmful. In a period of sustained declines in endowment market value, however, spending at a level independent of the value of assets could cause a loss of capital that would permanently damage the endowment fund.

A spending policy must be devised that addresses the conflicting objectives of preserving purchasing power and providing a stable flow of resources to the operating budget. Most institutions achieve the balance by determining a sensible long-term target rate of spending and applying that rate to a moving average of endowment market values.

Endowment Investment Philosophy

The tension between the goals of an endowment can be relaxed by investing for high rates of return. Hence, investing with an equity bias is the first tenet of endowment investment philosophy.

Finance theory indicates that acceptance of greater risk leads to the reward of higher expected returns. In a happy coincidence, historical data support the theoretical conclusion. Consider the following multiples for various U.S. asset classes from December 31, 1925, to December 31, 1992:[1]

Inflation	7.92×
T-bills	11.40
T-bonds	23.71
Stocks	727.38
Small-capitalization stocks	2,279.04

The data indicate that a $1.00 investment in Treasury bills at the end of 1925, with all income reinvested, would have grown to $11.40 at December 31, 1992. Given that $7.92 of that $11.40 would have been lost to inflation, that result is not particularly impressive. Thus, at least with 20-20 hindsight, Treasury bills would not have been an appropriate investment for an institution investing to earn substantial after-inflation returns.

Moving farther out the risk spectrum, the same $1.00 invested in longer term government bonds at the end of 1925 would have accumulated to $23.71 by the end of 1992. This performance, although much better than that associated with Treasury bills, is still not adequate for an institution that can consume only after-inflation returns.

In contrast to the bills and bonds, $1.00 invested in common stock would have accumulated to $727.38 during the 67-year holding period. The difference between the return expected from the conservative investments in cash ($11.40) or bonds ($23.71) and that expected from taking the greater risk in owning equity securities ($727.38) is enormous.

The long-term benefit of owning equities increases as investments are made farther out on the risk spectrum. For example, a $1.00 investment in small-cap stocks would have accumulated to $2,279.04 during the period, an impressive amount relative to $7.92 of inflationary drag.

The implication of these findings is that a long-term investor will maximize wealth by investing in the high-return, high-risk asset class rather than in the so-called conservative investments of Treasury bills and bonds. This conclu-

sion is somewhat simplistic, however, and requires further examination.

The following historical multiples for small-cap stocks show the behavior of security prices around the time of the 1929 Crash:[2]

November 30, 1928	1.00×
December 31, 1929	0.46
December 31, 1930	0.29
December 31, 1931	0.14
June 30, 1932	0.10

According to this data series, stock prices peaked in November 1928. Had $1.00 been invested at that time, it would have declined 54 percent by December 1929, an additional 38 percent by December 1930, an additional 50 percent by December 1931, and a final 32 percent by June 1932. From November 1928 to June 1932, $1.00 would have declined to $0.10. No investor, institutional or individual, can tolerate that kind of trauma. At some point during this period, when market forces turned dollars into dimes, investors would have sold their small-cap stocks, placed the proceeds in Treasury bills, and sworn never to invest in the equity market again.

This risk of placing all assets in one security type leads to the second tenet of endowment investment philosophy: Diversification is vital. The traditional response by most institutions upon recognizing the need for diversification is to put cash and bonds in the portfolio as diversifying assets. Various surveys indicate that 85–90 percent of U.S. institutional assets are currently invested in the traditional asset classes—domestic cash, bonds, and stocks. As much as 35–40 percent of assets are invested in domestic fixed-income securities and cash. Such a strategy is a high-cost approach to diversification. Money is being taken out of equities, where a dollar during the past 67 years has grown to $727 or $2,279 (for small-cap equities) and placed in cash or bonds, where the same dollar has grown to only $11 or $24.

Diversification without the opportunity costs of investing in fixed income can be achieved by identifying high-return asset classes that are not highly cor-

[1]*Stocks, Bonds, Bills, and Inflation: 1993 Yearbook* (Chicago, Ill.: Ibbotson Associates).

[2]*Stock, Bonds, Bills, and Inflation: 1993 Yearbook.*

related with domestic marketable securities. The most common high-return diversifying strategy for a U.S. investor is to add non-U.S. equities to the portfolio. Other possibilities for institutions are real estate, venture capital, leveraged buyouts, oil and gas participations, and "absolute return strategies" (that is, commitments to event-driven investments in merger or bankruptcy situations and to value-driven investments in long/short or market-neutral strategies). If these asset classes provide high, equity-like returns in a pattern that differs from the return pattern of the core asset (U.S. domestic equities), a portfolio can be constructed that offers both high returns and diversification.

Portfolio Construction

Investment returns are generated by decisions regarding asset allocation, market timing, and security selection. Portfolio construction must reflect the relative importance of the expected contribution of each source of return.

The most important source of portfolio return is that attributable to policy asset allocation. The process of selecting policy targets involves defining the asset classes that will constitute the portfolio and determining the proportion of assets to be invested in each class. The weights and market returns of a portfolio's various asset classes will determine the largest portion of a portfolio's returns.

The second source of return is market timing, defined as deviation from the long-term policy targets. For example, assume that a fund's long-term targets are 50 percent stocks and 50 percent bonds. A fund manager who believes stocks are cheap and bonds expensive during a certain period might weight the portfolio 60 percent to stocks and 40 percent to bonds for that period. The return resulting from the overweighting of stocks and underweighting of bonds relative to long-term targets would be the return attributable to market timing.

The third source of return, security selection, is the return generated by active management of the portfolio. If a manager created portfolios that faithfully replicated the markets (i.e., passive portfolios), that manager would be making no active bets. To the extent that a portfolio differs from the composition of the overall market, that portfolio has an active-management component. For example, security-selection return for the U.S. equity asset class would be the difference between returns from the U.S. equity portfolio's securities and returns from the asset class, as defined by a benchmark index of U.S. equities.

Comparing Sources of Return

When Brinson and Ibbotson studied institutional portfolio returns in the United States, they found that more than 90 percent of the variability of returns is attributable to asset allocation decisions.[3] Less than 10 percent of the variability of portfolio returns is attributable to market timing and security selection. Significantly, the overwhelming portion of *positive* contribution to returns stems from asset allocation. Market timing and security selection have marginal, and generally negative, contributions to portfolio returns.

Charles Ellis argues that market timing is a loser's game and essentially impossible to do on a consistent basis.[4] Ironically, nearly every institutional investor, by failing to rebalance to long-term targets, engages in market timing and, accordingly, allows portfolio risk and return characteristics to drift with the markets. Most portfolio managers take no action when their asset allocations vary as prices of one asset class change relative to the others. An example comes from experiences during the October 1987 crash in the world equity markets. In June, July, and August, most institutional investors simply watched their U.S. equity exposure increase as U.S. equity prices were rising and bond prices were falling. Of course, by October 1987, equity allocations of institu-

[3]Gary P. Brinson and Roger G. Ibbotson, *Investment Markets: Gaining the Performance Advantage* (New York: McGraw-Hill, 1987).

[4]References throughout to Mr. Ellis are to: Charles D. Ellis, *Investment Policy: How to Win at the Loser's Game* (Homewood, Ill.: Business One Irwin, 1993); see also Mr. Ellis's presentation on pp. 6–13.

tions peaked, just in time to experience a traumatic, more than 20 percent, decline. After the crash, not only did institutional investors fail to buy equities, which were now much cheaper on a relative basis, but those investors exacerbated the problem by being net sellers of equities in November and December. By failing to rebalance portfolios to long-term targets, most institutional investors ended up buying high and selling low, a poor recipe for success in portfolio management.

In efficient markets, active portfolio management, like market timing, tends to detract from aggregate investment performance. In the context of relative performance, security selection is a zero-sum game. If IBM represents 3 percent of the market value of the U.S. equity market, the only way an investor can hold an overweight position in IBM is for other investors to hold a corresponding underweight position in IBM. The active manager who overweights IBM will create market impact and incur transactions costs in establishing the position; on the other side of the trade are other active managers underweighting IBM, incurring those same transactions costs and creating market impact. Only one of those positions can be right when measured by IBM's future performance. The amount by which the winner wins will equal the amount the loser loses. The net result is that those investors actively managing their portfolios will lose as a group (by the amount of fees and market impact and transactions costs) relative to the market benchmark.

In highly efficient markets, a passive-management approach is appropriate. For example, investment managers should be completely passive in the Treasury bond market. In that market, perhaps the most efficient market in the world, the major relevant bet is on the direction of interest rates, an unknowable variable. Timing the bond market epitomizes Charles Ellis's loser's game.

In contrast, dealing with an inefficient market, such as the venture-capital market, requires intense active management. Intelligent application of investment principles is essential in determining whether to back the entrepreneur who may have the next biotechnology

wonder company or the programmer who has the software industry's next Microsoft. The passive alternative, a decision to back every entrepreneur's business plan regardless of quality, is certain to generate disappointing returns on investment. Active management is essential in inefficient markets.

Given the dominance of efficiently priced marketable securities in institutional portfolios, the conclusions about market timing and security selection reached by the Ibbotson and Brinson study are not surprising. The overwhelming contribution to return comes from the asset allocation policy decision; the contributions of market timing and security selection tend to be relatively minor and negative.

Implications for Portfolio Construction

These conclusions regarding the source of portfolio returns have important implications for portfolio construction. Construction of a traditional portfolio dominated by marketable securities must reflect a serious focus on the asset allocation decision. Market timing should be avoided, and the portfolio should be rebalanced regularly to long-term targets. Rebalancing imposes a discipline that results in buying low (after a decline in an asset's relative price) and selling high (after a rise in relative prices.) Finally, the decision to engage in active management should include serious consideration of the efficiency of markets. That is, active management of portfolios should be pursued primarily in less efficient markets and only if the fund manager is able to add value net of all costs.

A nontraditional portfolio attempts to achieve diversification by using alternative high-return assets, such as private equity, real estate, and absolute return strategies. Even with a nontraditional portfolio, careful definition of asset allocation targets is the most important function of an institutional fund manager. As in the case of traditional portfolios, market timing should be avoided; having more markets available to the portfolio manager does not increase the likelihood of being able to buy low and sell high.

The major difference in construction of a nontraditional portfolio is in active management of asset classes. Alternative assets, by their very nature, tend to be less efficiently priced than traditional assets. Managers should move into less efficient markets only if they consider themselves able to do a sensible job of actively managing those assets.

The return data for actively managed accounts for the past ten years for various asset classes can illustrate the differences in opportunities available in the classes. The difference between first-quartile returns and third-quartile returns shown in **Table 1** serves as a proxy for the degree of opportunity. In the bond market, the most efficient asset class, the difference between first- and third-quartile returns was 1.7 percent annually for ten years. In the venture-capital industry, the least efficient asset class, the difference was 12.2 percent annually. A much greater reward accrues to being in the first quartile in the venture-capital industry than to being in the first quartile in the bond market. Moreover, ironically, developing a strategy to achieve first-quartile results is much easier in the inefficient venture capital market than in the efficient bond market.

The Yale Experience

In Yale University's endowment, a matrix of expected return and risk levels for the relevant set of asset classes provides the framework for constructing an in-vestment portfolio. **Table 2** presents the policy asset allocation targets and expected return and risk characteristics for assets in the Yale endowment portfolio. Data for establishing policy targets are long-term (10–15 year) expectations for market conditions. The expected return levels are not precise point estimates of future conditions but represent the relative relationship among the various classes.

Asset Allocation

The U.S. equity portfolio is the core asset of the endowment. Although the allocation at 22.5 percent, is low relative to other institutions, U.S. equity is still the largest single asset class in the endowment. With an expected after-inflation return of 6 percent and expected standard deviation of 20 percent, equities should be the primary source of long-term growth for the endowment. The Wilshire 5000 Index, the broadest possible measure of market capitalization of the U.S. equity market, is the benchmark for the equity portfolio.

Non-U.S. equities, used primarily for diversification, have a 12.5 percent allocation in the fund. The expected return and standard deviation are identical to expectations for the U.S. equity market. Holding non-U.S. equities generates two benefits relative to investment in U.S. markets. The first is that active-management opportunities are greater in non-U.S. markets because non-U.S. securities are less efficiently priced. The second is that the emerging markets contain especially attractive opportunities. A number of developing

Table 1. Active-Management Returns: Ten Years Ending December 31, 1993

Asset Class	First Quartile	Median	Third Quartile	Range
U.S. fixed income	12.6%	11.9%	10.9%	1.7%
U.S. equity	16.8	15.5	14.1	2.7
U.S. small-cap, growth equity	18.4	16.4	13.3	5.1
Venture capital	11.9	6.3	–0.3	12.2

Sources: Data for fixed income, equity, and small-cap, growth equity are from the *Piper Managed Accounts Report* of December 31, 1993. The venture-capital data are from *Venture Economics.*

Table 2. Yale University's Asset Allocation Targets, Expected Return Characteristics, and Expected Risk Characteristics

Asset Class	Target Weight	Expected After-Inflation Return	Expected Risk (standard deviation)
U.S. bonds	15.0%	2.0%	10.0%
U.S. stocks	22.5	6.0	20.0
Non-U.S. stocks	12.5	6.0	20.0
Private equity	20.0	14.0	30.0
Absolute return	20.0	7.0	15.0
Real estate	10.0	6.0	15.0

Source: Yale University Investments Office.

countries, such as Mexico, Korea, and Malaysia, have the potential to grow their economies at substantially higher rates and provide more attractive investment opportunities than the developed countries. Offsetting the advantages of overseas investments are the higher associated costs. The portfolio benchmark is a weighted average of 85 percent of the GDP-weighted EAFE return and 15 percent of the International Finance Corporation Emerging Markets return.

Private equity, which accounts for 20 percent of the endowment, is included primarily for its high-return potential. Companies involved in leveraged buyouts (LBOs) are generally too similar to assets in the equity portfolio to provide much diversification. A somewhat stronger argument can be made that venture capital provides diversification. For example, the process of creating a company adds value that is largely independent of events influencing the marketable securities markets. Nonetheless, the main benefit of private equity is the contribution made by its expected real return of 14 percent (with a 30 percent risk level).

The absolute return portfolio is targeted to be 20 percent of the endowment. This portfolio uses a combination of strategies to exploit inefficiencies in the marketable securities markets with results that are substantially independent of stock and bond market movements. Included are activities such as merger arbitrage, convertible arbitrage, investment in distressed securities, and a range of market-neutral strategies. Generally, the in-

vestment horizon for these strategies is one-to-two years, with expected real returns of 7 percent representing a slight premium to those expected from domestic equities, albeit at a lower risk level (only 15 percent).

The fixed-income portfolio, at 15 percent of endowment assets, consists exclusively of long-term, high-quality, domestic, noncallable government bonds. Expected real returns are 2.0 percent (with a standard deviation of 10 percent). The bond portfolio is, in a sense, the anchor of the endowment. Bonds provide a hedge against deflation and financial accidents, such as a crash like that of October 1987. The benchmark for the fixed-income portfolio is the Lehman Brothers Government Bond Index.

Real estate, with a 10 percent allocation, is expected to generate returns commensurate with domestic equities and provide portfolio diversification. Bonds and real estate are the most powerful diversifying assets in the portfolio. Whereas bonds provide a deflation hedge, real estate is expected to hedge against unanticipated inflation. In past years, the price of real estate's diversifying characteristics was lower expected returns. In recent years, the ability to take advantage of opportunities created by the real-estate-related distress of many financial institutions has increased return expectations, currently 6 percent real return (with a 15 percent standard deviation). The benchmark for the real estate portfolio is the Frank Russell Property Index.

Investment Management

The primary focus of the investment management process at Yale is the annual policy review. Three types of decisions are important to the investment process: policy decisions, the long-term establishment of investment targets; strategy decisions, the intermediate-term implementation of policy; and tactical decisions, the short-term effort to add value through timing and trading.

Charles Ellis argues that policy decisions are most important, a position that is consistent with the findings of the Ibbotson and Brinson study. Strategy is more fun than policy, however, and tactics are even more interesting. Discussing whether Digital Equipment will do better than IBM is more engaging than having a colorless discussion of policy targets for various asset classes. Market timing can be discussed at a cocktail party; dealing with long-term expectations for the equity market is not an exciting topic. Despite their mundane nature, however, policy targets are the focus of the Yale investment process.

Yale applies the best available tools of modern portfolio theory to the policy target decision. Asset-class data, together with a covariance matrix, are used to conduct Markowitz mean–variance optimizations. Monte Carlo simulations are used to test the implications of investment and spending policies for a horizon of 50 years (reflecting the charge to be long-term investors).

Application of these portfolio tools without informed market judgment, however, would be futile. For example, a mean–variance optimization conducted in 1987 using historical data might have resulted in a portfolio allocated 100 percent to real estate. Quantitative analysis incorporating real estate's high historical returns and low variance would indicate an unreasonable allocation to that asset class. In contrast, an informed observer would recognize that real estate valuations in 1987 were overextended and would conclude that the asset class should be avoided, not emphasized.

Many market judgments stem from the Investment Committee, which meets quarterly. Two of the four meetings are devoted to a review of investment policy. At the spring meeting, Investment Committee members raise issues that should be analyzed in the annual study, and the committee is informed about issues the investment staff expects to incorporate in the policy review. During the summer meeting, the policy targets are reviewed, and any alterations to long-term strategy are considered at that time. The fall meeting reviews results of the fiscal year (July 1 through June 30), including performance reviews of the various asset classes and of the endowment as a whole. The winter meeting involves an exhaustive study of one of the fund's six asset classes.

The results of this process have been dramatic. Ten years ago, Yale had a traditional portfolio; 90 percent of assets were in U.S. stocks, U.S. bonds, and cash. Today, the portfolio is more efficient in a mean–variance context, with much higher expected returns and a substantially lower risk level than would be the case with a traditional portfolio. Moreover, as this transition from a traditional to a nontraditional portfolio occurred, Yale generated double-digit investment returns, which placed its endowment performance in the top 1 percent of institutional funds.

Conclusion

The process articulated in this presentation can assist any manager of institutional assets. The framework encourages investment practices designed to meet the immediate and long-term needs of any institution. Defining the purposes of the fund, articulating goals, and establishing an investment philosophy are prerequisites for developing rational portfolios.

Question and Answer Session

David F. Swensen

Question: Have you considered bonds denominated in non-U.S. currency as an asset class for endowment diversification? Also, what is your view on commodities?

Swensen: Substantial disagreement exists in the Investment Office at Yale about using non-U.S.-currency bonds in our portfolio. One staff member argues for adding foreign currency bonds from a mean–variance perspective. Such bonds would be an effective diversifying asset and, in mean–variance terms, would create a more efficient portfolio than now exists.

My response is that bonds play a special role in the portfolio by providing a hedge against deflation, but only domestic bonds can provide that hedge with certainty. As a U.S. investor, I have no idea what the value might be of a Japanese bond in the event of severe deflation in the United States. Much depends on the unknown associated movement in exchange rates. The fundamental diversification benefits of bonds (namely, deflation hedging) might well be lost if non-U.S. bonds were used as a substitute for domestic fixed-income assets.

Investment in alternative asset classes, such as commodities, is appropriate as long as the fundamental return factors can be identified and understood. The potential for value creation in a venture-capital or LBO investment is clear, but the intrinsic source of return from commodities is unclear. Yale's only commodity-like investments have been several participations in the oil and gas industry. In each case, the investment was not simply buying exposure to energy prices but, rather, backing entrepreneurs who would be able to create value above market-level results.

Question: Non-U.S. assets, which are 12.5 percent of your portfolio, entail significant foreign exchange risk. How do you view exchange risk in terms of the long-term perspective that your fund must maintain?

Swensen: We also have significant disagreement in the Investment Office with respect to hedging foreign exchange risk. The issue is whether, as a policy, hedging the currency risk in the non-U.S. equity portfolio makes sense. Implementing a consistent hedging program would probably cost 20–30 basis points annually. The only advantage of the currency hedge is a lowering of the annual standard deviation of returns. A long-term investor should not pay anything of consequence simply to lower the annual variability of returns. From a longer perspective, riding out the foreign exchange fluctuations with an unhedged position would be a superior strategy.

If currency movements could be predicted, the assessment would be entirely different. My attitude toward currencies, however, is the same as toward interest rates: Some macroeconomic variables simply cannot be predicted, and exchange rates fall in that category.

Question: When you change asset allocations, do you engage in market timing?

Swensen: The answer depends on how market timing is defined. My definition is: an explicit move from long-term policy targets based on and intended to take advantage of assumed superior knowledge about the misvaluation of an entire asset class. In that sense, we do not engage in market timing. When changing policy allocations, we move expeditiously but carefully, taking care not to create excessive market impact, from one set of policy targets to the newly adopted set.

When dealing with illiquid asset classes, we recognize that implementing a decision to pursue new targets can take a long time. In inefficient asset classes, only the most attractive opportunities should be pursued. Such opportunities present themselves irregularly and unpredictably; so patience is essential. Thus, increasing the private equity portfolio from 15 to 20 percent of the endowment, for example, could take years. When because of illiquidity in asset classes, portfolio weights cannot be adjusted directly to long-term targets, short-term assessments of relative value cannot be completely avoided. Those portions of our fund that cannot be immediately invested in the desired portfolio are invested in whatever liquid asset class seems most sensible. This decision is based on our best assessment of the relative value of various asset classes. The absolute return portfolio is frequently a logical candidate because it has had relatively high returns and a great deal of stability. At times, when opportunities appeared compelling, we have used marketable equities as a substitute for uninvested allocations to illiquid asset classes.

Question: Implementing U.S. equity strategies, managing exposure to emerging market equities, selecting private equity managers, dealing with an absolute return portfolio, and searching for investment opportunities in general seems to be a lot of work. How much do you rely on outside managers to manage parts of your fund?

Swensen: Our general approach is to hire the smartest, most effective external managers in the world to manage various parts of the portfolio. The primary exception is the bond portfolio, which is managed passively by an internal group of professionals. Occasionally, in cases where external management did not appear to be necessary, we have pursued investment opportunities internally. For example, after the October 1987 crash, we bought a portfolio of closed-end funds at substantial discounts to fair market value. This purchase exploited a skill that we thought we possessed, namely, identifying superior asset managers. That decision worked out well; the discounts closed, the market did well, and the managers did better than the market. That decision was also an exception, however.

Question: Do you micromanage your fund managers?

Swensen: Absolutely not. If we have confidence in an external manager, we let that manager do exactly the job he or she was hired to do without interference.

Question: Does your Investment Committee deal with all three levels of asset allocation—policy, strategy, and tactics? Do the committee and fund staff have the same or different "informed market judgments"?

Swensen: The Investment Committee deals with all aspects of endowment management but focuses seriously, although not exclusively, on policy asset allocation. The staff brings to the Investment Committee issues as diverse as the tactics of disposing of a substantial equity position acquired through a venture-capital success, the strategy of exploiting opportunities created by the Resolution Trust Corporation, and policy implications of various investment and spending programs. The Investment Committee is involved in the entire spectrum of investment activities.

Generally, the interaction between the staff and the committee involves a great deal of give and take. Having well-informed committee members and well-prepared staff is critical to the decision-making process.

Question: Unlike pension fund spending levels, which are determined exogenously, endowment funds decide their own spending levels. Please discuss how spending rules are decided and revised.

Swensen: The spending rule that we followed throughout the 1980s had a long-term target of 4.5 percent, the spending rate we thought would allow us to support current operations and maintain purchasing power of assets. Analysis of the 1950–93 period indicates that spending at 4.5 percent was, on balance, consistent with the maintenance of purchasing power.

In 1992, based on a fundamental conviction that we had developed a portfolio with a higher expected return and a lower level of risk than previously, we increased the spending rate from 4.5 to 4.75 percent. Such changes ought to be made infrequently, and only after serious deliberation.

Investment Policy for North American Pension Plans

Keith P. Ambachtsheer
President
K.P.A. Advisory Services, Ltd.

In response to an increasingly complex and volatile investment environment, investment policies for pension plans are evolving on a more businesslike or economic basis than in the past. Policy creation and implementation are enhanced by attention to such issues as quality management and cost-effectiveness.

Setting investment policy for pension plans has become more and more important as management of these assets has become increasingly complex and the investment environment increasingly volatile. As for other types of investors, pension plan investment policy should reflect a plan's objectives, constraints, preferences, and market expectations. The setting and implementation of policy should also reflect the latest thinking about management processes and organizational structure. This presentation discusses types of plan arrangements in North America, what the decisions are in managing pension funds, and how those decisions can be made in the context of the quality-management paradigm.

Defined-Benefit versus Defined-Contribution Arrangements

The two basic types of pension plans in North America are defined-benefit and defined-contribution (capital-accumulation) plans; the key distinction between them is how the benefits are defined. Defined-benefit pension arrangements are between the employer and employees. This type of plan provides the employee, upon retirement, a level of benefits based on a formula that is usually related to years of service, employee earnings, or some combination of the two. The level of benefit, which may be with or without postretirement inflation protection, is defined independently of the value of the plan assets. The defined-benefit pension plan caught on as an employee benefit after World War II and was dominant until the 1980s. Asset growth for these plans was tremendous between 1960 and 1985, averaging 20 percent a year, which was well in excess of general economic growth. Since the mid-1980s, growth in defined-benefit assets has slowed considerably

Defined-contribution pension arrangements started to become increasingly popular in North America in the mid-1980s. The various defined-contribution arrangements have grown at the rate of 20 percent a year since then and are expected to continue to grow at rates of that magnitude for the foreseeable future. Defined-contribution plans do not promise set levels of retirement benefits. Instead, the employee, often together with the employer, agrees to an annual contribution of money, usually a percentage of salary, into a capital-accumulation fund in the employee's name. The money, which clearly belongs to the employee, can be invested in any or some combination of several investment vehicles. The assets accumulate over time and are owned throughout the accumulation period by the employee. At the end of some investment period, the accumulation may be paid out as a lump sum, converted to an annuity, or converted into an investment account; that is, instead of accumulating, the monies start to "decumulate" at some time as they flow out of that account.

A defined-benefit arrangement is most likely to be offered by large corporations or various public-sector employers (states, provinces, national governments, cities, hospitals, and educational systems). The defined-contribution arrangement has become the primary pension plan for mid-size and small employers and will remain so for reasons of cost-effectiveness, simplicity, and portability. Even large corporate employers have begun to offer defined-contribution plans in addition to some basic defined-benefit arrangement. These factors will likely result in relatively high growth in defined-contribution assets, whereas funds in defined-benefit arrangements can be expected to grow only at the general rate of the economy (i.e., 5–8 percent a year).

Nonetheless, defined-benefit pension assets are massive asset pools representing a considerable force in the economy and the capital markets, and they will continue to play that role well into the next century. As shown in **Table 1**, defined-benefit-plan assets at the end of 1992 totaled $2.5 trillion in the United States and $250 billion in Canada (compared with defined-contribution assets of $900 billion and $150 billion, respectively).

Table 1. North American Trusteed Pension Assets, 1992
(billions)

Country	Defined Benefit	Defined Contribution
United States (US$)	2,500	900[a]
Canada (CAN$)	250	150[b]

Source: U.S. data are from *EBRI Quarterly Investment Report* (Washington, D.C.: Employee Benefit Research Institute, September 1993). Canadian data are from *Trusteed Pension Funds Financial Statistics* (Ottawa: Statistics Canada, 1993).

[a]Primarily corporate 401(k) plans.
[b]Primarily group and individual registered retirement-savings plans.

Key Decisions and Quality Management

Quality-management experts played a major role in organizing North American war production before and during World War II, but later found an audience in Japan that was more receptive to thinking through the application of quality management to the manufacturing sector than were postwar North Americans. North American industry did not become interested in these techniques until the 1980s, in response to the tough time they were having selling cars and electronics. They suspected their troubles might have something to do with quality management, and thus the movement, discipline, and understanding of quality management came back to the North American continent.

The quality-management concept has now moved beyond the industrial sector and is being used in various contexts in the financial services sector. Since about 1990, several investigators have been considering how these ideas and disciplines might be used to examine pension fund management in a fresh way and improve the industry's management practices.

The quality-management discipline is easy to remember. The approach involves a disciplined search for answers to four basic questions:
- Who are the customers?
- What do they want?

- How is the product or service best delivered?
- What is the best path to continuous improvement?

Who Are the Customers in Defined-Contribution Plans and What Do They Want?

In defined-contribution arrangements, the sole customers are the plan members; they are in the position of making their own investment decisions. They and their employers make contributions, which they can allocate among several different investment vehicles. Typically, these vehicles are selected by the employer and supplied by third-party investment management firms.

The assets accumulate to some value over time; at a later stage of the customer's life, the customer's concerns turn to what kind of pension can be purchased with that accumulation. Thus, the focus in defined-contribution arrangements is on growth of the plan member's assets and their eventual conversion into a postretirement payment stream.

The investment counselors working for defined-contribution customers must help them understand the trade-offs involved in the following considerations: the proportion of final earnings to be replaced at retirement, the required savings rate, the contribution rate that can be afforded each year, and the different return prospects associated with different asset mixes. At one end of the investment spectrum are guaranteed investment certificates, which are short-term, relatively sure investments; from that kind of instrument stretches a continuum of more and more risky investments.

The concept of investment horizon is important in defined-contribution plans. Each plan member has a unique time horizon, and the horizon changes over time. A young employee has a 30- or 40-year investment horizon; a 64-year-old employee may have a 1-year investment horizon. Risk, and thus the proper investment policy, relates to the length of investment horizon. Currently, the North American investment counseling industry is trying to decide how best to help millions of defined-contribution-plan members determine what the trade-offs are—the realistic combinations of savings rates, return assumptions, and projected income-replacement rates that, when integrated with social security payments, provide realistic options. Trying to help people who are not necessarily sophisticated investors understand those basic trade-offs and make decisions is a monumental challenge for the industry.[1]

Many industry observers wonder what will happen to a pension system that has a large defined-contribution component in which all the individual plan members are placed separately at risk and left to make their own fundamental economic decisions about savings rates and asset-mix policies. The longer term implications of that kind of retirement system are unclear.

Who are the Customers in Defined-Benefit Plans and What Do They Want?

Plan members are also customers in defined-benefit arrangements; their interest is primarily benefit security—the likelihood that the plan will deliver the promised benefits. The employers also have an interest in defined-benefit arrangements. An employer has a financial interest in how well its plan is performing. The employer is promising to pay pensions and is thus at risk; if the assets do not generate at least some minimum assumed rate of return, the employer must make up the shortfall.

If the assets generate a return higher than the assumed rate, of course, excess assets are created, but for whose benefit? An interesting debate took place in the 1980s on this question. The economic answer is that the excess assets should accrue to the party undertaking the risk—that is, the employer's sharehold-

[1]I do not pursue these issues further in this discussion; readers who want to pursue them should see the AIMR publication titled *Quality Management and Institutional Investing,* based on a conference with that title held October 12–13, 1993. The remainder of this presentation deals with the finance and investment issues related to defined-benefit plans.

ers (in the case of corporate plans) or the taxpayers (in the case of public plans). Therefore, these groups are also customers in defined-benefit plans.

If they are rational, the collective customers of defined-benefit pension plans want predictable benefits, low long-term funding costs, and predictable plan contributions in the short, intermediate, and longer terms. This list may seem straightforward, but it is not a realistic set of wants that can be met simultaneously, which creates a challenge for the industry. Understanding the balance sheet of a defined-benefit plan can help meet that challenge.

The balance sheet, an example of which is given in **Exhibit 1**, clarifies the fundamental economic, financial, and investment issues in defined-benefit plans. The term "pension deal" on the right side of the balance sheet refers to the arrangement between the employer and employee. Pension benefits can accrue in several ways. In North America, these benefits are usually related in one way or another to final earnings (the final year of earnings or the average of the last five years of earnings).

In most corporate retirement plans, no formal agreement exists for the post-retirement updating of pensions or increasing payments for inflation, whereas several public-sector plans contain such agreements. Many corporate plans have an understanding, however, that updates will be made on a "best-efforts" basis. Research into the updating of pensions after retirement shows that average up-

dates are 50–60 percent of inflation. A plan's update policy and experience are important characteristics for estimating pension liability, which is the present value of some projected stream of future benefit payments. The financial characteristics of those payments, which are then discounted back to today at some relatively risk-free discount rate, must be clearly understood in order to estimate how much pension debt is currently outstanding on the basis of the pension deal.

Exhibit 1 highlights another important policy decision that must be made in North America—the normal relationship between the value of the assets and the value of the liabilities. This relationship is called the plan's funding policy. For example, the decision could be made to have a pension plan that has an asset surplus on average, has an asset shortfall on average, or has approximately equal assets and liabilities over time. The North American pension regulatory authorities and actuarial professions have something to say about the decision, but considerable latitude still exists as to whether the plan will be conservatively or aggressively funded. In the North American context, the fact that the employer, whether public sector or corporate, has the option to fund conservatively or aggressively demonstrates a direct connection between the pension plan and other employer financial decisions. This aspect is what establishes pension plans as truly financial subsidiaries of their sponsoring employers.

Exhibit 1. Balance Sheet for a Financial Institution Servicing Pension Debt

Assets	Liabilities
What is the immunizing asset-mix policy?	What is the pension deal?
Should the actual asset-mix policy attempt to earn a spread over the return of the immunizing asset-mix policy?	How much pension debt is currently outstanding on that pension-deal basis?
How should the actual asset-mix policy be implemented?	**Surplus**
	By how much do assets exceed pension debt outstanding?
	By how much should assets exceed pension debt outstanding?

Source: Keith P. Ambachtsheer, *Pension Funds and the Bottom Line* (Toronto, Canada: Keith P. Ambachtsheer and Associates, 1992).

Defined-benefit plans are created in North America by issuing pension debt. The fact that pension debt is being issued and that, legally, that debt must be funded creates assets to be invested. Pension assets do not exist in some vacuum; in a balance-sheet context, they are clearly related to a financial entity that is in the pension business.

How Is the Product or Service Best Delivered?

Delivery of the pension "product" on the asset side of the balance sheet involves the setting of investment policy, fiduciary responsibilities, cost-effective organizational structure, and effective use of information, particularly in performance measurement.

Investment policy. Formulating investment policy in a pension fund that backs defined-benefit pension liabilities is a three-step process. The first step is to create an asset portfolio that mirrors the financial characteristics of the pension obligation (in duration, inflation sensitivity, and discount rate) in the characteristics of the asset (length, quality, and inflation sensitivity). This creation is called the "immunizing investment policy" in Exhibit 1. Realistic treatment of the pension liabilities makes finding an immunizing portfolio difficult. Nevertheless, an asset portfolio can be constructed with a reasonable resemblance to the liability portfolio. Knowing what that portfolio looks like is necessary before addressing the next step in the policy process.

The second step is to decide whether to try to earn a spread between the actual asset portfolio and the immunizing portfolio. Earning a higher rate of return than that assumed in the funding policy for the balance sheet has clear benefits, and a number of options will then exist. For example, the sponsor's contribution rate could be reduced, or the pension benefits could be increased.

If the decision is to attempt to earn such a return spread, the third step is to determine the actual asset-mix policy to be implemented. This determination cannot be made without understanding who is to make it, which introduces the role of fiduciaries.

Fiduciary responsibilities. If the three steps just described were all that is needed in deciding the investment policy of a defined-benefit pension plan, then the task would be conceptually easy. The three steps are not the essence of the task, however. The challenge comes from the fiduciary responsibility inherent in the investment decisions.

Managing in a quality context and trying to meet customer needs in a defined-benefit context place fiduciaries in the role of making decisions on behalf of the ultimate customers, namely, plan members and shareholders or taxpayers. The fiduciaries' decisions must be made in a way that constitutes a reasonable trade-off among the various customers' needs—benefit security, a low long-term funding rate, and no surprises about contribution volatility. Fiduciaries take on the responsibility for understanding the trade-offs and making appropriate decisions among the spectrum of all possible decisions. Because North America contains thousands of defined-benefit plans, thousands of bodies—investment committees or boards of directors—are charged with making these decisions.

Their first step, as noted previously, should be to identify the asset portfolio that looks like the liabilities. Their second and third steps are to decide whether to try to earn extra return over the long term, and if so, how much to target. Their fourth step is to address uncertainty in a positive way.

Fiduciaries can deal with uncertainty in four ways:

- assume there is no uncertainty; that is, ignore the question because it is too difficult to handle;
- assume the management of uncertainty can be delegated to investment managers;
- assume it can be precisely specified through probability distributions and covariances; or
- assume it can be approximated for the relevant time horizon by

postulating plausible capital market outcomes.

In a quality-management approach, the first two choices are nonstarters. To decide between the third and the fourth choices, the fiduciary needs to reflect on the appropriate and inappropriate uses of historical economic and capital markets data.

Although the investment policy process is forward-looking, historical return and risk information (in terms of mean return, volatility of return, and covariances) can provide valuable lessons to decision makers, but only if they avoid indiscriminately using history as the best future set of prospects. **Table 2** illustrates the problem with such use, namely, that histories are not random draws. Disaggregating the past 60 years into five time periods makes clear that stock and bond returns and the economy in different periods have very different experiences. For example, one factor that drove stock returns in each period, other than earnings growth and dividend growth, is how differently stocks were priced at the beginning and at the end of the period.

Understanding capital market history can be helpful in addressing uncertainty explicitly, not in some broad aggregate sense but in a more defined, era-specific sense. Thought about the next five or ten years must recognize that they are not just any five or ten years; they are the specific five or ten years that start in 1994, preceded by the specific history shown in Table 2.

One example of this type of prospective thought is given in **Table 3,** which contains the returns projected for different asset classes for 1994 through 1998. Table 3 is how one person sees the future from today's perspective. The base case, called "degearing," is an environment of relatively modest real GDP and inflation growth. This environment is stable in comparison with the possibilities of "deflation" or "inflation." Such a scenario approach is more manageable and transparent than struggling with future uncertainty through tracking 12 probability distributions and their joint covariances. That approach can easily deceive fiduciaries into believing the future is much more predictable than it actually is.

Organizational structure. Once investment policy has been decided, the next step is implementation. A key issue in effective policy implementation is organizational structure, and to understand its role requires understanding the factors that have led to current pension fund organizational structures.

One such factor is the evolution of the laws and accounting standards related to pensions. In North America, pension systems emerged from the trust banks and insurance companies in the 1950s, 1960s, and 1970s. Over time, the pension plans have become increasingly self-standing, self-managed, and autonomous financial institutions. They are governed by individuals or groups who willingly take on the fiduciary obligation to be responsible for the financial welfare of a plan within the constraints of the relevant legislation and court cases that help determine issues that were not clear in the original law. The result is that the pension sector in

Table 2. Summary of Historical U.S. Capital Markets Experience

Item	Depression/ Deflation (1928–40)	Wartime Controls (1941–51)	Pax Americana (1952–65)	Inflation (1966–81)	Disinflation (1982–90)
Real GNP growth	0.8%	5.1%	3.3%	2.8%	2.8%
Inflation	−1.6	5.8	1.4	6.9	4.1
Stock return	−2.0	13.7	14.5	5.9	16.1
Nominal real	−0.4	7.9	13.1	−1.0	12.0
Bond return	5.6	0.7	1.2	1.3	16.0
Nominal real	7.2	−5.1	−0.2	−5.6	12.1
Bill return	1.4	0.7	2.7	7.3	8.4
Nominal real	3.0	−5.1	1.3	0.4	4.3

Source: The Ambachtsheer Letter, No. 91 (Toronto, Canada: KPA Advisory Services, January 14, 1994).

Table 3. Projected Returns for Different Asset Classes, 1994–98

Item	Degearing	Deflation	Inflation
Real GDP growth	2.50%	1.0	3.0
Inflation	3.00	1.0	6.0
Nominal returns			
T-bills	4.50	2.5	6.5
T-bonds	6.25	7.5	2.0
Stocks	8.25	−8.0	2.0
Real returns			
T-bills	1.50	1.5	0.5
T-bonds	3.25	6.5	−4.0
Stocks	5.25	−9.0	−2.0

Source: The Ambachtsheer Letter, No. 92 (Toronto, Canada: KPA Advisory Services, February 1, 1994).

North America, unlike the case in Japan, is now viewed as separate and distinct from the banking and insurance sectors.

Pension fund organizational structures have also been shaped by other factors. Conley and O'Barr, for example, studied pension fund managers using anthropological research techniques and reported results that were not kind to the pension fund management community.[2] The authors began with the assumption that some clear economic rationale would explain why a pension fund is organized the way it is; instead, they determined that culture, diffusion of responsibility, and blame deflection are the main motivators for pension fund organization. A fund might be organized in a particular way because 20 years ago a problem occurred, someone was fired for it, and a set of systems was created to make sure the problem never happened again. The results also indicated that determining who is responsible for decision making is difficult because organizing for diffusion of responsibility is widespread. In addition, organizational structures were found to be influenced by the desire of managers to be able to deflect blame onto someone else if something goes wrong.

North American pension fund managers reacted angrily to these findings, scoffing with disbelief and attempting to discredit the authors for both their motives and their lack of understanding of such a technical area. To some degree, the criticisms were appropriate, but the research served the pension fund managers well because it focused on the important issues of why funds are organized as they are and how organizational structure can be reexamined to improve pension fund management.

In the context of customer wants, the only defensible rationale behind a fund's organizational structure is cost-effectiveness. Cost as a motivation for organizing refers to that level of resource allocation that creates the appropriate balance between what resources cost and what they are likely to deliver in investment performance. A focus on cost-effectiveness places the motivation in the economic arena rather than some noneconomic arena.

Until pension funds started measuring operating costs, this industry had no basis for estimating operating costs and no way of knowing whether the resources devoted to managing assets made any economic sense in relation to the value produced. Only in recent years have some sensible numbers on operating costs been developed. Based on estimates made by Cost Effectiveness Measurement, the direct, visible operating costs of North American pension funds in 1992 were about $10 billion.

Another aspect involved in delivering the pension product is serious examination of resource allocation to active and passive management. The entire pension fund need not be actively managed; the only certainty about the pension fund that is 100 percent actively managed is that it will be more expensive than one that is not; the actively managed fund is not guaranteed to generate a higher rate of return net of costs.

---

[2] John M. Conley and William M. O'Barr, *Fortune and Folly: The Wealth and Power of Institutional Investing* (Homewood, Ill.: Irwin Professional Publishing, 1992).

So, the economic issue in deciding the appropriate level of active management must involve some analysis of the marginal value of research and the fund's ability to implement active strategies compared with the costs of those processes. Out of that analysis will come some idea of what proportion of assets should be actively managed.

Since the introduction of the Wells Fargo Index Fund in the early 1970s, an increasing percentage of pension assets in North America has been placed under passive management. Today, about 40 percent of pension assets are passively managed, which means that fees are not 50 basis points but 5 basis points for a significant portion of North American pension assets.

Similar issues exist in the decision to use internal management or external management. Before the 1970s, an individual pension fund would have few suppliers. Gradually, however, this situation changed; today, many large North American pension funds have as many as 40 outside investment managers, 3 custodians, and 4 different consultants performing different roles.

Management of all these suppliers can be very difficult, which coupled with the shift to an economic rationale for decision making, has led many large funds to reevaluate their use of outside suppliers. The goal is to determine which services can and should be done internally and to determine the most effective ways to buy those external services that are needed. Many large North American pension systems now manage a considerable portion of their assets internally; the very large funds may be 80–90 percent internally managed.

One result of quality management for many manufacturing firms has been a radical redefinition of their relationships with suppliers. As the same kinds of issues are addressed in the context of pension fund management, the funds will be focusing on

- a small number of key strategic relationships with global suppliers of investment management, execution, custodial information, and advisory services and

- a number of additional relationships with niche suppliers offering a variety of specialty services.

Information. The measurement of operating costs allows proper performance measurement—that is, the comparison of costs incurred and returns produced relative to some established policy. With a large enough data base, such analysis also allows assessments of what one firm is spending and earning compared with what another firm is spending and earning. These assessments can convey a sense of how cost-effectively a pension fund is being managed and can provide a track to follow in defining and measuring cost-effectiveness.

Formal performance measurement of asset returns was given its impetus in 1968 when the Bank Administration Institute published its study of measuring the investment performance of pension funds.[3] The major message of this study was that, if performance numbers in the pension industry are to be comparable, the timing of different cash flows must be standardized. The industry has learned since this study that other performance measures also need to be standardized. For example, to be consistent with the notion of cost-effectiveness, the essence of performance measurement should be an assessment of the relationship between incremental return and incremental cost. So, the measurement process should focus on the meaning of incremental return and incremental cost in relation to appropriate benchmarks.

The implication is that, once a policy has been decided, a return proxy must be generated for that policy. The proxy should be the return the policy would produce if it was implemented in the most broadly diversified and passive (lowest cost) way. The difference between the actual fund return and the policy return can be defined as the implementation return—the contribution of management, whether more than or

---

[3]Peter O. Dietz, *Measuring the Performance of Pension Funds* (Park Ridge, Ill., BAI, 1968).

less than the policy return, to total return. Measuring incremental returns is one example of the kind of measurement that needs to evolve in support of an economic approach to asset management.

What is the Best Path to Continuous Improvement?

Continuous improvement relies on an ability to identify and measure the "right things" at each step of the management process. In pension fund management, customer needs are clear; thus, managers want to measure the factors that will increase their chances of delivering the desired bundle of services.

Measuring the right factors requires regular reviews of the balance sheet. Because balance sheets like the one conceptualized in Exhibit 1 now exist in a computerized form and can be updated annually at little cost, a manager can see at a glance what is happening to the assets and liabilities, why the assets or liabilities are growing, and how much investment policy and the method of implementation are contributing to or detracting from performance. These factors become the regular focus of strategies for continuous improvement.

An example of a very disciplined quality-management approach is given in **Figure 1.** This manager of a $15 billion pension fund has established four areas for continuous improvement: the balance of active and passive investing, asset allocation, organizational structure and supplier relationships, and benchmarking processes. Benchmarking in this case refers to analyzing the best implementation practices in the industry and measuring the fund's performance by those benchmarks. The manager has set priorities for making improvements on the basis of the potential cost-effectiveness impact of an improvement and the difficulty in achieving improvement. For example, the Figure 1 rankings indicate that this manager believes the easiest and most effective improvement will come from changes in the active–passive split.

Figure 1. Improving Policy Implementation

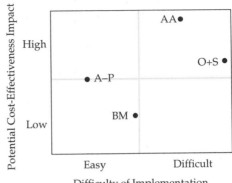

Key:
A–P = Active–passive split
AA = Asset allocation
BM = Benchmarking the process
O+S = Organizational structure and supplier relationships

Source: Based on a presentation by Thomas J. Cowhey, "Pension Fund Management: Quality Management Perspective I," to the Quality Management and Institutional Investing Seminar, Toronto, Ontario, Canada, October 12–13, 1993.

Based on this analysis, the manager did indeed change this fund's split from 100 percent active management to about 70 percent active management. The manager then reported that cost improvements were clear without any loss on the return side.

The same disciplined approach to thinking about pension fund management as a business can be applied at the level of the individual investment management firm. **Figure 2** presents the key attributes of continuous improvement in an investment management firm to be improving research, improving the implementation of research ideas, improving benchmarking of the process, and improving the interface between the investment management firm and its clients. This process focuses the firm's attention on continuous improvement and the relative difficulty of getting better in the four critical areas.

Conclusion

The North American pension fund industry is moving toward managing the $3 trillion of assets for defined-benefit

**Figure 2. Improving Investment Firm
           Management**

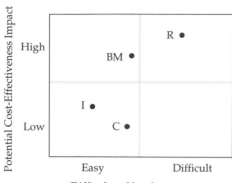

Key:
I   =   Research-idea implementation
BM   =   Benchmarking the process
C   =   Client interface
R   =   Research that potentially adds value

Source: Keith P. Ambachtsheer, based on Figure 1
framework.

plans on a more businesslike or economic basis than in the past. Investment policies are being determined by explicitly struggling with the uncertain trade-offs between immunizing pension assets or trying to raise long-term return so that funding costs will decline.

In implementation, the emphases are on the most cost-effective way of implementing the chosen investment policy and on the measurements necessary to determine and monitor cost-effectiveness and the effectiveness of individual portfolio management processes.

With its focus on customers and their wants, the quality-management discipline can improve future pension fund management by providing insights useful to both policy creation and implementation.

Question and Answer Session

Keith P. Ambachtsheer

Question: When deciding the percentage of active and passive portions, how can managers measure improvement in a quantitative manner?

Ambachtsheer: With a good deal of humility. Managers are making judgments related to issues about which they can never be quantitatively sure. What we can say fairly, however, is that most investment managers with large asset pools typically do not actively manage the entire stock and bond portfolios. Say we find approximately 75 percent is passive and 25 percent is truly active. An obvious cost-effectiveness question in such a case is why the fund should pay an active management fee on both the 25 percent that is truly active and the 75 percent that is effectively the core portfolio and that can be replicated simply by an index fund. In such a case, the 75 percent may well be worth only 5 basis points in fees, whereas the other 25 percent is worth a higher active-management fee.

The other consideration is the appropriateness of fee structures. Some pension fund managers have gone to performance-based fees—a structure in which the fee is some low base plus some participation in performance. This approach is almost an automatic way of paying passive fees only when the fund is getting passive performance and paying a passive fee plus a higher fee when the fund is actually earning an incremental active return. In short, different ways exist of dealing with the question of making improvements through changes in the active–passive split, one of which is to consider the fee structure, although the question will never have a precise quantitative answer.

Another aspect of active versus passive management, one raised by Perold and Salomon, is whether an investment manager's capability of generating a certain amount of excess return is independent of the amount of assets under management.[1] In other words, if a manager can generate an alpha of 5 percent a year with $100 million, can that manager generate the same alpha of 5 percent a year with $1 billion or with $10 billion? The answer at some point is no. The important issue is the relationship between certain strategies and the optimal size of assets that should be managed under those strategies. Analytical work to determine what may be the optimal size helps the plan think about the trade-offs between manager styles and the optimal size of assets under management.

Question: Do you have ideas about how to decide and manage a pension fund's tolerance for uncertainty?

Ambachtsheer: All investment programs have a context; they do not exist in isolation. For example, the risk-tolerance question needs to be addressed quite differently depending on whether it relates to a defined-contribution plan or a defined-benefit plan. In the former case, individuals must make their own decisions. As I noted in my presentation, for a defined-benefit plan, among the parties potentially at risk are plan members. They are faced with the possibility of default if the assets are not large enough to cover the benefit promises made to them and if the shareholders

---

[1] André F. Perold and Robert S. Salomon, Jr., "The Right Amount of Assets under Management," *Financial Analysts Journal* (May/June 1991).

(in the private sector) or taxpayers (in the public sector) fail to make up the difference. If plan sponsors do make up the difference, they are bearing the financial risk of sponsoring the pension plan. Thus, collectively, both the plan members and the plan sponsors are at risk. The challenge is to sort out the nature of those risks and to decide which parties should bear how much of the total risk embodied in the plan.

Remember also that these decisions are not made by the stakeholders directly but by agents on their behalf. Agency theory deals with the question of how to motivate agents to act appropriately on behalf of the parties for whom they are agents, with whom they have a fiduciary relationship. The difficulty of the motivational task is increased because these types of decisions are not made by the pension fund manager but by an investment committee or a board of directors or trustees. The real challenge, then, is for pension fund managers to present the appropriate information to the fiduciaries. The fiduciaries must be informed so that they can exercise their responsibility to make knowledgeable, even-handed decisions.

The case study illustrates this issue. Given some information and background about a public-sector and a corporate pension plan, funding levels, and risk tolerances, you, as the pension fund managers in the case, must make recommendations about investment policies to the boards. Just as no completely mechanical answer can be prescribed to the question of the active–passive balance, so no mechanical answer exists to the question of appropriate investment policy. It is based ultimately on an informed discussion among fiduciaries who understand what their fiduciary obligations are.

Fiduciaries need to see information that relates directly to the ultimate customers, such as the degree to which a policy places plan members and shareholders or taxpayers at risk. The answers may be different for a well-funded public-sector sponsor or very profitable corporate plan sponsor from what they are for a financially weak plan sponsor. The former may be able to bear more risk than the latter, which may require a conservative investment policy. Whatever information is generated should reflect a businesslike, analytical process that keeps the customers (shareholders or taxpayers and plan members) in mind.

Question: Your discussion of Table 2 implied that the five-year economic picture for assessing likely future risk and return on the asset side should be updated periodically—possibly as often as every year—to take into account the changing environment. The pension fund liability is much longer. How do you reconcile the gap between the liability-side time horizon and the asset-side time horizon?

Ambachtsheer: Part of the reason for assessing risk on the asset side for shorter horizons than the full liability horizon is, in fact, to assess the long-run viability of the plan. In many situations, five years is a long enough period that significantly adverse investment experience will have a significant impact on plan contributions. I do a lot of my work in five-year planning periods that are updated every year. Every year begins a new five-year period, and the end of the horizon is never reached.

To the extent that an investment policy may result in such significant adverse effects on assets and have a financial impact on the plan sponsor (by forcing higher-than-expected contributions), that policy is of significant importance to the sponsor. In North America, the tendency has been to force increasingly fast funding in plans that have become underfunded. Previous 30- or 40-year amortization periods have been replaced by five-year periods. Five years of adverse experience can, therefore, create a considerable asset shortfall that must be made up in a relatively few years. Five years is not always the appropriate period, but these kinds of considerations are what determine the length of the planning period for investment policy; the planning period is that period of time during which significant adverse experience would have a significant financial impact on those bearing the risk.

Question: Despite the fact that interest rates were recently declining and had been for some time, most of the actuaries still use 8 percent discount rates. Should we change the asset-side assumptions even though the liability assumption has not been changed?

Ambachtsheer: This question has been the subject of discussion in North America in the past six months. Using 8 percent discount rates for the liability seemed appropriate for quite some time. Suddenly, long-term interest rates dropped 200 basis points, but nevertheless, the tendency was to continue using 8 percent—until the Securities and Exchange Commission intervened to question this practice. Everybody had to go back to the drawing board and start using more realistic numbers. The SEC's position is consistent with the idea of managing an economic balance sheet, in which the assets and liabilities are comparable numbers. If they are not comparable, then the resulting set of asset and liability numbers makes risk analysis and the assessment of pension plan performance difficult, if not impossible.

U.S. and Japanese Pension Policies

John R. Thomas, CFA
President and Chief Executive Officer
J.P. Morgan Trust Bank, Ltd.

The finding that assets are priced similarly in Japan and the United States allows evaluation of Japanese pension plans within the framework of the evolving U.S. approach to setting pension policy. The funding status of Japanese plans varies greatly, and Japanese plans in general appear to be underfunded by U.S. standards.

A considerable part of my 30 years of experience working with U.S. pension plans was devoted to helping clients answer their most commonly asked question: "What is the correct asset mix for our pension fund?" This presentation seeks to share this experience, which has been augmented by a year's exposure to the pension industry in Japan.

The specific issue is whether the U.S. approach to setting pension policy applies in Japan. The presentation will address this issue by, first, briefly summarizing the evolving U.S. approach; second, sharing some research results about Japanese capital markets and the usefulness of capital market theory for yen investors; third, examining the opportunity set available today to Japanese pension plans; and finally, providing a look at the financial status of Japanese pension plans, with an opening illustration of the method that uses detailed information about J.P. Morgan–Tokyo's pension plan.

U.S. Pension Plan Policy

For many years, from the beginning of the industry through the 1950s, pension plan policymakers in the United States believed assets should be invested primarily in low-risk fixed-income securities (bonds). These views began to change in the 1960s. In the many heated discussions at J.P. Morgan about what the investment policy should be, the prevailing answer was to invest more money in stocks. By 1972, 80 percent of J.P. Morgan's typical balanced pension portfolio was invested in U.S. stocks.

The next two years were extremely painful because the U.S. stock market declined 50 percent; during the same period, returns on small-company investments declined almost 80 percent. In 1973 and 1974, therefore, dissatisfaction with stock market performance created great interest in capital market theory, and this interest coincided with the passage of ERISA (the Employee Retirement Income Security Act of 1974). These two factors were the major forces for increased diversification of pension plan assets.

Diversification followed two trends. The first was investment in a broad range of specialized asset classes, such as international investments, real estate, and so forth. The second, related, trend was the hiring of many new investment managers with a variety of skills and styles. Both trends focused only on assets; liabilities—that is, the promise to pay future benefits—were generally ignored. Indeed, liabilities were not well understood by those setting investment policy.

Pioneers, however, were developing new techniques. In the past 15 years, the prevailing approach has been to look at assets and liabilities together in an integrated fashion. Computer models have become available that enable pension plans to examine the impact of various investment policies and economic scenarios on specific plans. All of these approaches are based on one overriding belief: that the plan sponsor, investment managers, and all other organizations and individuals working with the pension plan are fiduciaries and have a responsibility to serve the undivided interest of pension plan participants. Fiduciary responsibility assures that the pension benefits earned by workers for 12, 30, or 40 years will be paid when they retire.

Today, corporations consider their pension plans to be liabilities like any other financial liability. Plans represent promises to make future payments for many years. In today's integrated approach, plan sponsors need to know the "economic" liability of their pension plans (that is, the liability as calculated by using economic data, not statutory assumptions). The calculation of economic liability relies on "best estimate" actuarial estimates and capital market assumptions, and it will differ from the liability calculated by the actuary for funding purposes. Investment policy should reflect the best way to finance the economic liability.

To analyze these issues in relation to Japanese pension plans requires a general idea of how Japanese capital markets price different assets. If pricing is similar to that in the U.S. markets, the U.S. approach may be helpful to Japanese policymakers.

Japanese Capital Markets

The figures in this section compare data from extensive analyses of risks, returns, and correlations among major asset classes available to U.S. and Japanese investors. The calculations are from the standpoint of a dollar investor and a yen investor for roughly a 15-year period.

Four figures depict the frequency distributions of rates or returns based on annualized monthly data. **Figure 1** shows annualized monthly inflation rates in the United States and Japan (as reflected in each country's consumer price index [CPI]) from January 1979 through December 1993. The distribu-

Figure 1. Comparison of U.S. and Japanese Distributions for Inflation, 1979–93

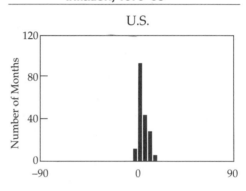

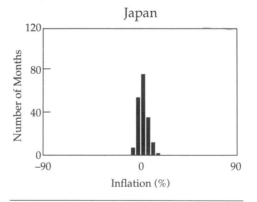

Source: J.P. Morgan.

tions for dollar-based and yen-based investors are fairly tight; these inflation rates have exhibited little volatility. For 94 months of the period, inflation in the United States was between zero and 5 percent. The data for Japanese inflation indicate 75 observations between zero and 5 percent. **Figure 2** provides the

Figure 2. Comparison of U.S. and Japanese Asset Return Distributions for T-Bills and Call Market, 1979–93

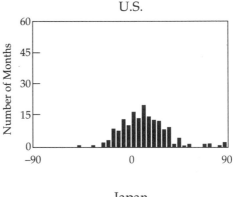

Figure 3. Comparison of U.S. and Japanese Asset Return Distributions for Medium-Term Bonds, 1979–93

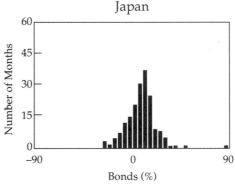

Source: J.P. Morgan.

Source: J.P. Morgan.

distributions for short-term interest rates—T-bills in the United States and call (overnight) market instruments in Japan (used as equivalent to short-term U.S. T-bills). The distributions are similar to those for inflation; T-bill returns were between 5 and 10 percent for 113 months, and call market rates were between 5 and 10 percent in 107 months.

Figure 3 shows the distributions for medium-term U.S. T-bond returns and for Japanese medium-term bonds as indicated by the Nomura Research Institute Bond Index. **Figure 4** follows the same approach as the first three figures to report distributions of stock market returns. The U.S. stock returns are from Ibbotson Associates' *Yearbook,* and the Japanese stock returns are returns to investing in the Tokyo Stock Exchange Index adjusted for total return, including dividend yield. Japanese bonds are significantly more volatile than instru-

ments in the call market, and stocks are much more volatile than bonds. The Japanese bond distribution shown in Figure 3 is broader than the call market distribution in Figure 2 but is not nearly as broad as the stock distribution in Figure 4.

The distribution patterns are similar for the U.S. and Japanese investor for inflation and short-term investments. The Japanese bond distribution (Figure 3) is narrower than the U.S. distribution; bond volatilities in Japan were lower in this period than in the United States. Stock distributions for both countries are very wide. The large spikes on the right of each graph in Figure 4 are actual observations above the 90 percent outer boundary of the graph. The conclusion from this series of figures is that the volatility patterns of similar assets are comparable in the United States and Japan.

The next figures reveal the risk and return characteristics of major asset classes

Figure 4. Comparison of U.S. and Japanese Asset Return Distributions for Stocks, 1979–93

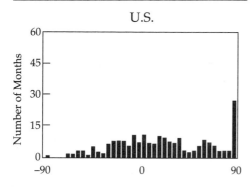

Source: J.P. Morgan.

Figure 5. Historical Standard Deviations of Annual Returns of Major Asset Classes for U.S. Investors, 1978–93

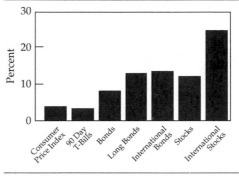

Source: J.P. Morgan.

for the United States and Japan. The time period used for U.S. assets is January 1978 through December 1993, and for Japanese assets, January 1979 through December 1993. The choice of time periods was based on ease of data collection and does not affect the conclusions.

Figure 5 shows the standard deviations (risks) of annual returns, unhedged, of major U.S. asset classes. The standard deviations range from below 5 percent for T-bills to more than 13 percent for long bonds (U.S. Treasuries) and international bonds. Volatility for U.S. stocks was about 12 percent, and for international stocks (based on the EAFE Index), 25 percent. The pattern of rising volatility by asset class for this period is generally consistent with long-term history; the only possible surprise is that U.S. stocks were less volatile than bonds.

Figure 6 shows the returns of major asset classes for U.S. investors. Looking at Figures 5 and 6 together reveals that one premise of capital market theory (higher risk receiving higher return) was generally upheld in this period. With one slight exception (international bonds had greater risk but lower return than U.S. stocks) those assets with greater risk also garnered higher returns.

Figure 6. Historical Annual Rates of Return of Major Asset Classes for U.S. Investors, 1978–93

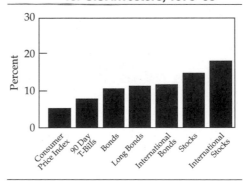

Source: J.P. Morgan.

Figure 7 reveals the Japanese risk experience, and **Figure 8** shows historical returns of major Japanese asset classes. The risk–return picture is not nearly as neat as that for the U.S. market, but in general, the higher risk assets achieved greater returns. Reward/variability is interesting because of substantial differences among asset classes. In the call

Figure 7. Historical Standard Deviations of Annual Returns of Major Asset Classes for Yen Investors, 1979–93

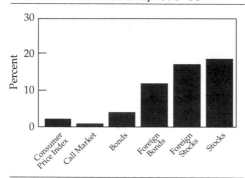

Source: J.P. Morgan.

market, return was 6 percent, so volatility of 0.6 gives a reward-to-volatility ratio of 10; the ratio for bonds was about 1.9, and for domestic stocks, 0.5. U.S. asset classes examined on the same basis do not reflect nearly such a wide range of volatility.

Figure 8. Historical Annual Rates of Return of Major Asset Classes for Yen Investors, 1979–93

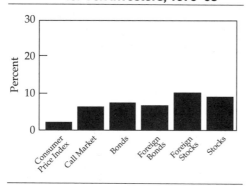

Source: J.P. Morgan.

The correlations between pairs of asset classes in the United States and Japan for the study periods are given in **Table 1**. Note the negative correlations for Japan in the case of call market returns with domestic stock returns and the case of domestic stock returns with international bonds. The correlation between returns for the Japanese call market and domestic bonds is positive but less than 0.2.

The conclusion based on Table 1 is that correlations during the period be-

Table 1. Correlation Coefficients of Annual Returns

Asset Classes	United States	Japan
T-bills (call loans) and domestic stocks	0.22	(0.04)
T-bills (call loans) and domestic bonds	0.75	0.10
Domestic stocks and domestic bonds	0.52	0.26
Domestic stocks and international stocks	0.45	0.23
Domestic stocks and international bonds	0.29	(0.07)
International stocks and international bonds	0.69	0.63

Source: J.P. Morgan.

Note: The period for the United States is 1978 through 1993; for Japan, 1979 through 1993.

tween pairs of Japanese (yen) asset classes were lower than those between comparable U.S. asset classes—particularly for the call instrument versus bonds or stocks. The Japanese call rate has been quite inelastic; only in the past few years has it dropped significantly and shown increased volatility. U.S. money market investments have been linked much more closely with U.S. stocks and U.S. bonds. Within each country, correlations between domestic stocks and domestic bonds were meaningful. The correlation between international stocks and bonds was high from the perspective of either a dollar or yen investor.

This analysis gives rise to several observations. First, ranking asset classes by risk is similar whether one is looking at Japan or the United States. Liquidity-type investments have much lower volatility than fixed-income investments, which have much lower volatility than equity investments. Also, the distributions of returns for each asset class are comparable. Second, higher risk assets have earned higher long-term rates of return in Japan than in the United States, but reward volatility has been significantly different. Third, correlations among asset classes are lower in Japan, although the patterns in the countries are similar. These data and this analysis indicate that the capital markets in Japan and the United States price assets in reasonably similar ways.

Opportunities for Japanese Pension Plans

What risks and returns are the Japanese capital markets offering to investors today? This examination of the current risk–return opportunity set for Japanese pension plans raises some interesting questions for pension plan sponsors and Japanese regulators.

Rates of return for major asset classes currently available in the Japanese markets and forecasted volatility of the major asset classes are shown in **Table 2**. In contrast to the preceding discussion, Table 2 assumes fully hedged

Table 2. Approximate Capital Market Returns and Future Risks for Yen Investors

Asset Class	Annual Rates of Return	Annual Standard Deviations
Call market	2.50%	1.0%
Bonds	4.00	5.0
International bonds	5.00	6.5
International stocks	7.25	13.5
Stocks	7.00	15.0

Source: J.P. Morgan.

international assets, with roughly a 2.5 percent annual cost for hedging through purchasing forward currency contracts. Call market rates today are actually lower than the 2.5 percent estimated in the table, and the Japanese bond yield on a compounded annual basis is probably a little below the 4 percent shown. The long-term forecast is that Japan's equity market is priced to provide about a 7 percent annual rate of return.

The risk and return forecasts combined with the correlation coefficients produce the efficient frontiers depicted in **Figure 9**. The frontiers were constructed under three different parameters: subject to the 5-3-3-2 regulation with and without investment in foreign

Figure 9. Efficient Frontiers for Yen Investors

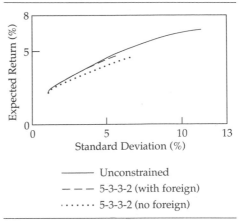

Unconstrained
— — — 5-3-3-2 (with foreign)
⋯⋯⋯ 5-3-3-2 (no foreign)

Source: J.P. Morgan.

securities, and unconstrained.[1] The unconstrained efficient frontier was formed by letting an optimizer select whatever it wanted for the portfolio, and it illustrates what the risk–reward trade-off could be if the current asset-mix guidelines were removed.

The maximum-return portfolios would provide an expected 4.9 percent return with a standard deviation of 6.3 percent for the regulated/with foreign investment portfolio and an expected return of 5.3 percent with a standard deviation of 6 percent for the regulated/no foreign investment portfolio. Clearly, under the current 5-3-3-2 guidelines, having the ability to invest internationally provides greater efficiency than not having that ability. An unconstrained portfolio, however, would provide an expected return of 7.2 percent with a standard deviation of 11.9 percent. An unconstrained portfolio would greatly extend the opportunity set. If a fund were interested in taking on more risk, it would have the opportunity to achieve somewhat higher returns.

The probabilities of achieving the required 5.5 percent annual rate of return over five years from the maximum-

[1]Under current regulation in Japan, plan sponsors must construct portfolios with a minimum of 50 percent in Japanese fixed-income instruments, a maximum of 30 percent in Japanese equities, a maximum of 30 percent in foreign securities, and a maximum of 20 percent in real estate.

return portfolios were as follows: under current regulations, 39 percent if not invested in foreign investments and 44 percent if foreign investments are included. The unconstrained portfolio would increase the probability of achieving this return to 58 percent.

The expectations, if valid, have significant implications for the ability of Japanese pension funds to provide adequate returns to fund existing pension plans. Investment managers face a real challenge in dealing with realized-gain requirements. The situation is, in many ways, almost a classic mismatch. That is, a fund may want to take the higher risk portfolio in order to have a better chance of achieving higher returns over time. But the fund is expected to realize an absolute 5.5 percent return every year. Economically, that constraint works against the best interests of the beneficiaries of the portfolio. It can cause a fund manager to alter investment style. If a fund manager must make a 5.5 percent realized-gain return every year, that manager may not be able to adhere to a long-term style. The pension liability is one of the longest liabilities a company can have; so, constraints that force the pension fund to focus solely on annual results create a classic mismatch in durations of assets and liabilities.

Another factor is that transaction costs in Japan are high; so, anything that causes investment managers to transact merely to realize gains will unnecessarily reduce the ultimate returns for a long-term portfolio.

Financial Status of Japanese Pension Plans

To set the stage for a discussion of the financial status of Japanese pension plans on an *economic* basis, the status of U.S. funds will first be discussed. The economic funded status reflects the market value of the assets divided by the market value of the liabilities. **Table 3** shows the economic funded status of 200 major U.S. pension plans at year-end 1987 and year-end 1992. In each case,

Table 3. Economic Funded Status of 200 Major U.S. Pension Plans

Funding Quintile	1987	1992
Top	156%	143%
Middle	117	105
Bottom	86	81

Source: J.P. Morgan.

pension assets are valued at market values. Liabilities are discounted at current market rates.

As Table 3 shows, the funded position of the top, middle, and bottom 20 percent of pension plans deteriorated to some degree between 1987 and the end of 1992. U.S. pension fund participants can, in general, expect that the promised benefits from their pension plans will be paid, although those whose pension funds are in the bottom 20 percent may have some reason to be concerned.

J.P. Morgan–Tokyo will be used to illustrate calculation of the economic status of Japanese pension plans. J.P. Morgan–Tokyo, with only 500 employees, is a small entity compared with many Japanese organizations. Roughly 50 percent of the plan's assets are managed by insurance companies. Its economic financial status based on local regulations is as follows: Assets are valued at book value, ¥2.2 billion. The pension liability is calculated using the required "entry age normal" actuarial cost method, with the standard actuarial assumptions for all Japanese companies of a 5.5 percent rate of return and a 5.5 percent discount rate. The result is a ¥3.2 billion pension liability. On a statutory basis, the J.P. Morgan–Tokyo pension plan is 69 percent funded, well below the economic funded status of the lowest 20 percent of U.S. companies and well below the funded status of J.P. Morgan's pension plans worldwide.

This statutory liability can be compared with various pension liabilities the plan would have under different assumptions. One alternative, although it is not realistic, illustrates how things can change: Continuing to use the entry-age-normal method and best-estimate actuarial assumptions for salary growth, employee turnover, future return, discount rate, and so forth, would cause the liability to jump to ¥6.6 billion—more than double the statutory liability.

Another liability estimate is found if the actuarial cost method is changed from entry age normal to projected unit credit, the method used in the United States under Financial Accounting Statement (FAS) No. 87. Using the same best-estimate actuarial assumptions used in the first alternative and the 5.5 percent discount rate, this second alternative provides a pension liability of ¥3.6 billion.

Calculations for a third alternative would be the same as for the second except that a 4 percent discount rate is used, which is about the current market rate for the "benchmark" Japanese government bond. This rate change causes the liability to increase to ¥5.1 billion.

In summary, if the assumptions and approach most used and accepted in the United States are applied to the J.P. Morgan–Tokyo pension plan, the economic liability of the plan is significantly higher than the statutory liability—¥5.1 billion versus ¥3.2 billion. The plan assets valued on the basis of economic principles have a ¥2 billion market value as opposed to the ¥2.2 billion book value. With plan assets at ¥2 billion and under the most likely economic assumptions, the funded status of the J.P. Morgan–Tokyo pension plan is 39 percent or 56 percent or somewhere in between.

Many differences could exist between Japanese funds and the pension plan for J.P. Morgan–Tokyo, a foreign company, that would create this type of low economic funded ratio. One difference is that large portions of the benefits provided by Japanese pension plans are taken on a lump-sum basis, which dramatically alters the duration pattern of the liabilities. That portion would be much lower for J.P. Morgan.

The approach used to analyze J.P. Morgan–Tokyo's pension plan was used to create **Table 4**, which gives the results of an analysis of data for 21 Japanese corporate pension plans based on the 10-K forms they provided to the SEC under FAS No. 87 regulations when they filed security offerings offshore. The average economic funded ratio (the funded status according to FAS No. 87) for the 21 plans was 60 percent. Of these companies, one pension plan was only 40 percent funded on an economic basis and one was 128 percent funded. Obviously, if the current market rate of 4 percent were used, the funded status of all these plans would be worse than shown in Table 4. These substantial differences in funded status exist despite the fact that all these plans are governed by the same regulations, actuarial assumptions, and so forth.

Conclusion

In general, the principles of capital market theory appear to apply in Japan, and the odds are high that this applicability will increase in time as financial deregulation and globalization of capital markets continue.

Based on available data, Japanese pension plans are apparently underfunded on an economic basis. Under capital market expectations, the prob-

Table 4. Economic Status of 21 Japanese Pension Plans

Plan Description	Average of 21 Pension Funds	Plan with Lowest Funded Ratio	Plan with Highest Funded Ratio
Market value of assets (billions)	¥135	¥63	¥79
Economic pension liability (billions)	224	158	62
Funded ratio	60.0%	40.0%	128.0%
Discount rate assumption[a]	5.5	5.5	5.5

Source: J.P. Morgan.

[a]Seventeen companies used 5.5 percent; one company used 5.0 percent; two companies used 6.0 percent; and one company used 7.5 percent.

ability of these plans achieving the required 5.5 percent annual rate of return with the current asset-mix regulations is less then 50 percent. One could argue that those with fiduciary responsibility should strive to do what is best for the plan participants. Therefore, intensive examination of the financial status of each pension fund in Japan seems essential.

Question and Answer Session

John R. Thomas, CFA

Question: What would the funded status for the 21 Japanese plans be if calculated using the Japanese rather than FAS No. 87 standards?

Thomas: In going through Japanese annual reports, I did not find pensions to be a regular accounting item. This lack of available information for Japanese pension plans is why I used the J.P. Morgan–Tokyo approach.

A Tale of Two Pension Funds: Case Study (A)

Jim Jones, the chief financial officer of the Alpha Corporation, one of America's largest manufacturing companies, and Barbara Smith, the chief investment officer of the Public Sector Retirement System (PSRS), a large state retirement system, were having lunch together in February 1994 at the Tiffany restaurant in New York City. The two friends were in New York to attend a conference on the future of the U.S. capital markets. They had both been involved in investment management for pension funds for more than 25 years and had attended numerous such conferences.

During lunch, Smith and Jones agreed that the investment of pension fund assets had grown increasingly complex during their careers in the business and that the challenges were likely to increase in the future. They also discussed the outlook for the U.S. capital markets for the balance of the decade and the implications of that outlook for their respective pension funds. The discussion was particularly timely because both managers had to make formal presentations to their boards of directors or trustees within the coming two weeks regarding potential changes in their pension funds' strategic asset allocations.

The Role of Pension Funds in the U.S. Capital Markets

In the United States, the development of the pension fund industry was essentially a 20th century phenomenon. American Express founded the first private pension

Note: Case series and analyses prepared by Keith P. Ambachtsheer; Richard D. Crawford; and Donald L. Tuttle, CFA. Based on Keith P. Ambachtsheer, "Pension Fund Asset Allocation: In Defense of a 60/40 Equity/Debt Asset Mix," *Financial Analysts Journal* (September/October 1987):14–24, and Letters Nos. 91, 92, and 93 of *The Ambachtsheer Letter* (respectively, January 14, February 1, and February 11, 1994).

plan in the United States in 1875.

Since World War II, pension funds had grown rapidly, to the point that they were by 1994 major factors in U.S. and global capital markets. Between 1950 and 1993, the growth rate of pension assets exceeded that of the GNP by more than six times. In 1950, 2,000 pension plans were operating in the United States, with $17 billion in assets and covering 25 percent of the U.S. work force. By 1974, when ERISA (the Employee Retirement Income Security Act) was signed into law, the number of pension plans had grown to 50,000, with total assets of $200 billion, and the plans were covering 50 percent of the work force.

Following the adoption of ERISA, which emphasized risk in a total portfolio context rather than in individual investments, pension funds began to diversify into nontraditional assets, such as real estate, international securities, and venture capital. This move, combined with stringent funding requirements and strong stock and bond returns, fueled further pension-asset growth, and in the 19 years following ERISA, total pension fund assets had increased more than 22 times. During the especially rapid growth period of the 1980s, pension fund assets grew at an annual compounded rate of 12.5 percent. By the end of 1993, more than 37,000 corporate, union, and government pension funds in the United States had total assets of $4.44 trillion, a sum greater than the country's national debt and approximately equal to the total assets held by life insurance companies, thrift institutions, mutual funds, and money market funds combined.

Of the $4.44 trillion in pension assets, private pension funds controlled $2.26 trillion. Insured pension assets (those managed in insurance company general accounts) totaled $935 billion. State and local government funds and other assets held in U.S. government plans amounted to $1.25 trillion.

By the end of 1993, pension funds owned approximately 40 percent of U.S. companies' equity capital and more than two-thirds of the equity capital of the 1,000 largest U.S. businesses. Pension funds were the primary suppliers of equity capital in the United States and were also major sources of debt financing, particularly long-term debt financing. By the year 2000, pension funds were expected to hold at least two-thirds of the share capital of all U.S. businesses (excluding the smallest firms) and, therefore, to be even more significant in the overall investment environment than in 1994.

U.S. pension plans can be assigned to one of two major categories: defined-benefit plans and defined-contribution plans. Defined-benefit pension plans promise specified benefits, typically in the form of a monthly retirement pension, based on levels of compensation and years of service. Defined-contribution plans require a specific contribution on behalf of each participant, usually expressed as a percentage of compensation and normally unrelated to employer profits, and leave the benefits unspecified and largely dependent on the performance of the portfolios in which employees invest the contributions.

The Alpha Corporation and PSRS Pension Plans

Jones and Smith were responsible for making investment decisions for two defined-benefit pension funds with significantly different characteristics. Even if they agreed on the outlook for capital markets, therefore, the differences in their pension funds might lead the two to make substantially different asset allocations. In fact, each pension fund had historically pursued dissimilar investment strategies. The Alpha Corporation pension plan had used a 70 percent equity/30 percent debt asset mix, with the equity component diversified among a broad spectrum of domestic common stocks, venture capital, real estate, and foreign stocks and the debt component invested in long-duration, high-quality bonds. The PSRS pension plan had used a 50 percent equity/50 percent debt asset mix, with the equity component diversified similarly to the Alpha Corporation pension fund and the debt component invested in medium-duration, high-quality bonds.

Governance of the pension fund for which Jones served as chief investment officer was under the control of the Alpha Corporation; as set forth by ERISA, investment policy was conducted within the context of prudence and due regard for the obligation to maintain plan solvency. The plan was totally noncontributory on the part of employees and was being funded by the company on a 7.5 percent/5.5 percent basis (that is, the contribution calculations assumed a 7.5 percent investment return and a 5.5 percent growth in wages), which led to an 8 percent (of compensation) "normal" contribution rate. Benefit accruals were based on a formula that used average salary paid during the last several years prior to an employee's retirement; thus, projected benefits to be paid were related to future rather than to current earnings.

In addition, ad hoc postretirement "updates" (benefits not included in the contractual benefit formula) were paid on a discretionary basis by the Alpha Corporation board, with a target benefit increase based on 60 percent of the increase in the U.S. consumer price index (CPI). The plan made no explicit link between pension fund performance and the inflation updates. Updates increased the contribution rate only when the updated funding target exceeded the value of plan assets. The contribution rate was reduced if plan assets exceeded the funding target by a certain percentage. That is, because postretirement updates were strictly ad hoc or discretionary, even though a "target" increase of 60 percent of the increase in the CPI existed, Alpha Corporation did not prefund for the updates and, therefore, an inflation rate assumption was not critical in determining the company's contribution rate.

The investment policy of the PSRS pension plan that Smith supervised was similar to those of other public-sector defined-benefit pension plans. Investment risks and rewards were shared by the taxpaying public and active public-sector employees. The government and employees contributed to the plan on a 50 percent/50 percent basis. In the event of a shortfall of funds to pay the plan's obligations, increased contributions from the government and from active workers would be used to make up the shortfall. The composition of the PSRS board of trustees reflected the diversity of interested parties.

The PSRS plan benefits were based on final annual salary; because inflation effects would be reflected more fully in the final annual salary than in the average of several years' salaries, the benefits paid by the PSRS plan were more fully indexed than benefits in the Alpha Corporation plan. In addition, postretirement updates were explicitly tied to the CPI, with updates being 100 percent of CPI growth up to a maximum of 8 percent a year. Because of the need for prefunding of postretirement updates, an inflation rate assumption was quite important for the PSRS pension plan, and accordingly, the "normal" contribution rate was significantly higher than that for Alpha Corporation. The plan was being funded on the basis of 7.5 percent/5.5 percent/4.0 percent (nominal investment return/wage growth/inflation assumption), leading to a 16 percent (of compensation) "normal" contribution rate. Of the total 16 percent, the state (i.e., taxpayers) contributed 8 percent of pay and active plan members contributed 8 percent of pay.

A Template for Pension Fund Management

The two fund managers held similar views on major pension-fund-management issues. Smith and Jones both used the template of a pension-debt-servicing financial institution shown in **Exhibit 1** as the framework for their discussions. In this framework, the starting point for analysis is a clear understanding of the kind of pension debt the institution is servicing, the "true long-term contractual pension arrangement" or pension "deal" on the "Liabilities" side of the template.

Jones and Smith believed investment strategy should be based primarily on a "going-concern" view of the pension plan. In a hypothetical windup, or termination, of a plan, pension debt or liabilities could be valued using current interest rates as discount rates without any projections of increases in wages and prices. For a going concern, however, that approach does not provide a realistic valuation; thus, Smith and Jones believed that the importance of potential future wage and inflation experience had to be formally recognized in valuing pension liabilities.

On a going-concern basis, the market value of the assets of Alpha Corporation's pension plan now exceeded the estimated value of its pension debt by a modest amount. Alpha Corporation hoped to maintain this modest asset cushion as a hedge against the need to increase its pension contributions immediately in the case of adverse investment experience. In contrast, in the PSRS, liabilities now exceeded pension assets by a significant amount. The state government had agreed to reduce this unfunded liability, however, by making additional payments into the fund during the next 30 years.

Both fund managers believed the ideal asset-mix strategy to immunize their pension funds against going-concern pension liabilities (see the "Assets" side of Exhibit 1) called for appropriate proportions of fixed-rate bonds, inflation-sensitive bonds, and some equities to hedge against long-term trends in real wages. They viewed the essence of establishing an appropriate long-term investment strategy for their respective funds to be determining the size of "spread" to attempt to earn in excess of the return provided by this ideal immunizing investment strategy. Attempting to earn such a spread involved taking some balance-sheet risk beyond the risk posed by the immunizing asset strategy. That additional risk carried with it the risk that additional contributions into

Exhibit 1. Balance Sheet for a Financial Institution Servicing Pension Debt

Assets	Liabilities
What is the immunizing asset-mix policy?	What is the true long-term contractual pension arrangement, or pension "deal"?
Should the actual asset-mix policy attempt to earn a spread over the return of the immunizing asset-mix policy?	How much pension debt is currently outstanding on the basis of that arrangement?
How should the actual asset-mix policy be implemented?	**Surplus**
	By how much do assets exceed pension debt outstanding?
	By how much should assets exceed pension debt outstanding?

Source: Keith P. Ambachtsheer, *Pension Funds and the Bottom Line* (Toronto, Canada: Ambachtsheer and Associates, 1992).

the fund would be needed in the event of adverse investment experiences. If the riskier investments earned a higher rate of return, of course, they would have the opposite effect, which would reduce required contribution rates in the long term. To address fully these risk and return considerations, the two pension managers had to assess the likely future experiences of the capital markets.

Performance History of the U.S. Capital Markets

Jones and Smith knew that the performance of portfolios with different asset mixes could vary dramatically in different economic and capital market scenarios. For example, the history of the U.S. capital markets since the 1920s could be divided into several distinct periods, and performance of portfolios with the same mix of stocks and bonds had varied greatly from period to period. The two managers thus firmly believed in the importance to effective investment decision making of understanding underlying economic trends and other forces affecting the capital markets.

Jones and Smith agreed that the history of the U.S. capital markets since the 1920s could be divided into six major eras: 1928 through 1940, 1941 through 1951, 1952 through 1965, 1966 through 1981, 1982 through 1990, and 1991 to the

present. They believed that the 1990s had ushered in a new era in the U.S. capital markets but were not sure when it would end—or even how it would develop.

During the six decades between 1930 and 1990, financial assets had generally produced positive returns. The three major asset classes (stocks, bonds, and bills) had all outpaced the rate of inflation. According to Ibbotson Associates,[1] in the 1926–92 period, stocks, bonds, and U.S. Treasury bills had average annual returns of 10.3 percent, 4.8 percent, and 3.7 percent, respectively. During this 66-year period, the average annual inflation rate was 3.1 percent; therefore, stocks, bonds, and bills had real average annual returns of 7.2 percent, 1.5 percent, and 0.6 percent, respectively. Real annual U.S. GNP growth averaged 2.8 percent.

Although the real returns for the entire period were positive for the three asset classes, real returns for different asset classes in the different major historical periods had varied greatly. The reason was diverse impacts on the different assets of a number of factors, including inflation and deflation. **Table 1** summarizes the real and nominal returns for different asset classes in the different historical periods.

The 1928–40 period was marked by

---

[1]*Stocks, Bonds, Bills and Inflation: 1993 Yearbook* (Chicago, Ill.: Ibbotson Associates).

Table 1. U.S. Capital Markets Experience in Five Eras

Item	1928–40	1941–51	1952–65	1966–81	1982–90
Real GNP growth	0.8%	5.1%	3.3%	2.8%	2.8%
Inflation	−1.6	5.8	1.4	6.9	4.1
Stock return (nominal)	−2.0	13.7	14.5	5.9	16.1
Stock return (real)	−0.4	7.9	13.1	−1.0	12.0
Bond return (nominal)	5.6	0.7	1.2	1.3	16.0
Bond return (real)	7.2	−5.1	−0.2	−5.6	12.1
Bill return (nominal)	1.4	0.7	2.7	7.3	8.4
Bill return (real)	3.0	−5.1	1.3	0.4	4.3

Source: The Ambachtsheer Letter, No. 91 (January 14, 1994).

the stock market crash of 1929, the Great Depression, and deflation in the economy. Overall during this period, real U.S. GNP growth was only 0.8 percent annually and the inflation rate was a negative 1.6 percent annually. This deflation hammered returns on stocks while making returns on bonds very attractive. Real stock, bond, and bill returns during the period were, respectively, −0.4 percent, 7.2 percent, and 3.0 percent.

The 1941–51 period was marked by the military buildup associated with World War II, the conversion of the economy to a civilian economy after World War II, price controls, and the Korean War. During this period, real GNP growth was 5.1 percent annually and the inflation rate was 5.8 percent annually. The general growth in the economy helped stocks in this period; the increase in inflation and the federal government's policy to put a ceiling on interest rates hurt bonds and bills. Real annual returns on stocks averaged 7.9 percent; real annual returns on bonds and bills averaged −5.1 percent.

The 1952–65 period was an era of American dominance in the world and great growth in economic prosperity. During this period, real GNP growth in the United States was 3.3 percent annually and the inflation rate was 1.4 percent annually—a combination that led to significant increases in Americans' real incomes. The financial markets benefited from the general increase in prosperity: The stock market experienced a great bull market in the 1950s, and real stock returns were 13.1 percent. Bond and bill returns during the period were −0.2 percent and 1.3 percent, respectively.

Fueled by growing federal government deficits that resulted from the military demands of the Vietnam War and the expansion of domestic social spending for the Great Society programs of President Lyndon Johnson, the 1966–80 period was marked by growing inflation and steadily rising interest rates. By the end of the 1970s, U.S. interest rates had soared to previously unreached high levels. Overall during this period, real GNP growth was 2.8 percent annually and the annual inflation rate was 6.9 percent. Financial assets suffered from the poor performance of the economy and growing inflation; real annual stock returns averaged −1.0 percent, and real annual bond returns averaged −5.6 percent. Real annual T-bill returns were slightly positive at 0.4 percent.

The 1981–90 period was marked by disinflation in the U.S. economy as the Federal Reserve tightened the money supply under the leadership of Paul Volcker and Alan Greenspan. This period also included massive federal government deficits because reductions in tax rates by the Ronald Reagan administration were accompanied by a massive military buildup in the first half of the 1980s and a failure to cut social programs and entitlements. During the period, real U.S. GNP growth was 2.8 percent and inflation was 4.1 percent. This period was one of prosperity, however, for financial assets and financial markets. Real annual stock, bond, and bill returns averaged 12.0 percent, 12.1 percent, and 4.3 percent, respectively. This period was also marked by the globalization of capital markets, with significant integration of the financial and currency markets in the North America–

Europe–Japan triad and the savings and investment transformation in the East Asia bloc (which, including India, accounted for 40 percent of the world's population). Aggregate investible financial capital and stock market capitalization approached $1 trillion in the East Asia bloc.

Although no definitive conclusions were yet possible, projections for the new era beginning in 1991 and lasting beyond the year 2000 were for real U.S. GNP growth of 2.5 percent annually and average inflation experience of 3.0 percent. Real returns on bills might be about 1.5 percent annually; on bonds, 3.25 percent; and on stocks, 5.25 percent. This new era was expected to be a time of "degearing" of private- and public-sector balance sheets to more sustainable relationships between income, debt, and equity than had been the case in the recent past.

Outlook for Capital Markets

As their lunch progressed, Jones and Smith discussed their five-year predictions for the U.S. and global capital markets. Because both approached their pension plans as going concerns, capital market prospects were very important. The money to make benefit payments came only from contributions to the pension funds and investment earnings on those contributions. The greater the investment earnings, therefore, the lower the level of contributions required.

Jones and Smith foresaw three possibilities for the direction of the capital markets in the United States for the balance of the decade: a base-case degearing scenario, an inflation scenario, and a deflation scenario. Both managers believed the degearing scenario was the most likely. Of the other two scenarios, Jones believed inflation was the more probable whereas Smith believed deflation was the more likely.

Smith described the degearing scenario as an extended period of relatively low output growth and low inflation in the North America–Europe–Japan triad. In this scenario, the U.S. capital markets

would have a relatively low interest rate structure, which would be reinforced by a broadly held perception that the experiences of the 1930s (deflation) or the 1970s (inflation) would not recur. Key market trends in this scenario would include the further global integration of financial markets, a continuing active market for mergers and acquisitions, and a rising demand for financial assets by maturing Baby Boomers in the United States.

Jones believed that the alternative inflation scenario might be beginning in the cyclical revival of the economies of the North America–Europe–Japan triad. The U.S. economy in 1994 was already in a recovery from the 1990–92 recession, and Europe and Japan were likely to recover from their recessions in the near future. This revival could strain resource supplies, and the resulting demand pull would ignite inflation. In addition to the effect of a general recovery in the triad, Jones expected two factors to reinforce the likelihood of the inflation scenario. One was the continued buildup of public obligations in North America and Europe at a rate exceeding general economic growth, with resulting increases in public debt in relation to GDP. The other was a possible global confrontation of the triad with either the former Soviet Union or the orthodox Islamic bloc, which would lead, respectively, to remilitarization or energy shocks.

The growth of public debt in North America and Europe was not an idle worry in 1994. A number of stories in the U.S. media had addressed the bankruptcy of the European welfare systems and the efforts of several European countries to cut benefits. In the United States, President Bill Clinton had introduced major legislation to provide universal health care insurance and services, and the respected Congressional Budget Office had just released a report indicating that the cost of the Clinton administration proposals would be substantially higher than administration estimates.

The possibility of global confrontation was also not an idle worry. Russia was in serious economic trouble, and although Russia's reform-oriented president, Boris Yeltsin, was still in office, recent parliamentary elections had favored Russian nationalist parties. The ongoing civil war in the Bosnian province of the former Republic of Yugoslavia provided a potential flash point for U.S.–Russian confrontation.

Similarly, the ongoing threat of militant Islam was underscored by growing attacks by radical Muslims on Western tourists in Egypt, traditionally one of the more moderate Islamic states. With world oil prices at very low levels (to the point that Saudi Arabia was experiencing cash flow difficulties), an increase in militant Islamic activity in key Persian Gulf states and a resulting rise in oil prices would have a seriously adverse impact on the world's economy.

Smith, on the other hand, believed that the economy of the United States had been degearing in the period between 1991 and 1994 and might stay in that mode for the balance of the decade. An extreme extension of degearing could occur, however—a deflation scenario—which would be led by a collapse of the Japanese economy and would spread to other countries of the triad as trade imploded and demand dropped.

Speculation about a potential trade war between the United States and Japan was widespread in 1994. Trade talks between the two countries aimed at reducing the trade imbalance between them had been unsuccessful. This development reinforced fears about the Japanese economy that had been highlighted in an article in the *Wall Street Journal* by Kenichi Ohmae, director of McKinsey & Company in Tokyo and one of the world's leading corporate strategists.[2] Ohmae discussed how Japan had become a very-high-cost manufacturer and, as a result, had suffered a loss of its advantage in international trade, how depressed real estate values in Japan could lead to trillions of dollars of future write-downs by Japanese corporations and financial institutions, and how Japanese markets for such consumer durables as autos and electronic products had become saturated.

Implications of the Capital Market Outlooks for Investment Policy

Although Jones and Smith had different outlooks on the likelihood of the scenarios, they agreed that all three could happen and believed they should analyze the potential impact of each scenario on their portfolios. They wanted to analyze the different effects on the returns of various portfolio asset classes in detail to clarify what the potential overall returns would be, given the historical equity/debt allocations of their funds, in the different scenarios.

Jones had already developed a preliminary estimate of asset-class returns, which is shown in **Table 2**. In making these projections, he had assumed that the occurrence of either the deflation or inflation scenarios would result in a significant correction in the equity markets.

Jones and Smith had some critical decisions to make before they could

---

[2]"Will Tokyo Fiddle While Japan Burns?" *Wall Street Journal* (January 19, 1994).

Table 2. Projected Returns for Different Asset Classes by Scenario, 1994–98

Item	Degearing	Deflation	Inflation
Real GNP growth	2.50%	1.0%	3.0%
Inflation	3.00	1.0	6.0
Nominal returns			
T-bills	4.50	2.5	6.5
T-bonds	6.25	7.5	2.0
Stocks	8.25	−8.0	4.0
Real returns			
T-bills	1.50	1.5	0.5
T-bonds	3.25	6.5	−4.0
Stocks	5.25	−9.0	−2.0

Source: The Ambachtsheer Letter, No. 92 (February 1, 1994).

complete their formal presentations to their boards of directors or trustees:

- Were the return prospects projected by Jones in Table 2 realistic?
- If those return prospects were realistic, what asset mix should they recommend?

To answer the second question, Jones and Smith agreed that, at a minimum, they needed to calculate the returns for at least four potential asset allocation strategies for each of the three economic scenarios. The four strategies to be analyzed were:

- 70 percent equity/30 percent debt,
- 60 percent equity/40 percent debt,
- 50 percent equity/50 percent debt, and
- 40 percent equity/60 percent debt.

The cash allocation would be zero in each strategy. In making these calculations, the two managers agreed that they should assume that each of the three economic scenarios has a reasonable chance of occurring. What asset allocation strategy do the results of these calculations suggest?

A Tale of Two Pension Funds: Case Study (B)

Jim Jones and Barbara Smith had a broad discussion of several recurring questions that affected their roles as chief investment officers of their respective pension funds. One topic was the state of capital market prospects over time. For instance, would the historical structure of risk premiums paid to investors continue in the future? A second topic was "ownership" of investment gains and losses: How should pension fund gains and losses be distributed between plan sponsors and plan beneficiaries? If the plan were to be terminated, would beneficiaries be paid only the legal minimum or a greater sum? A third topic was the value of plan assets and liabilities: Should the pension plan managers be concerned with short-term fluctuations in the economic value of plan assets and plan liabilities?

The answers to these questions were likely to have major impacts on the allocation of plan assets among different asset classes. In particular, Smith and Jones wondered whether one solution to the potential problems of changing risk premiums and short-term economic fluctuations might be the use of real-return bonds in their portfolios. Real-bond returns were indexed to inflation rates, so the interest and principal received by the holders of such bonds were fixed in real terms—that is, in terms of the purchasing power of the interest payments and the principal. Real bonds were attractive for managing exposure to pension fund liabilities with an inflation component. Because these liabilities were obligations stretching from the near term to many years in the future, any inflation adjustment in pension benefits created vulnerability to inflation. Real bonds solved this problem by allowing the hedging of inflation-indexed pension obligations with inflation-indexed assets of similar maturity. A number of governments, including those of Canada and Great Britain, were already offering real-return bonds, and other governments, including the U.S. government, might follow suit in the future.

To determine the potential impact of real bonds in their portfolios, Jones and Smith would have to calculate the return on a new set of appropriate asset mixes for each of the three economic scenarios. The five asset-mix strategies they decided to analyze were:

- 70 percent equity/30 percent fixed-rate debt/0 percent real-debt,
- 50 percent equity/50 percent fixed-rate debt/0 percent real-debt,
- 40 percent equity/40 percent fixed-rate debt/20 percent real-debt,
- 0 percent equity/40 percent fixed-rate debt/60 percent real-debt allocation,
- 0 percent equity/20 percent fixed-rate debt/80 percent real-debt allocation.

The cash allocation was zero in all strategies.

Jones and Smith agreed that, in making these calculations, they would assume that the real returns on real bonds would be 2.5 percent annually in the degearing scenario, 0.0 percent in the deflation scenario, and 3.7 percent in the inflation scenario. The nominal returns would be 5.5 percent, 1.0 percent, and 9.7 percent, respectively. They further agreed that they would assume that each of the three economic scenarios had a reasonable chance of occurring. What asset-allocation strategy do the results of these calculations suggest?

A Tale of Two Pension Funds: Case Study (C)

Having discussed and developed approaches to deal with the impact of different economic scenarios on their asset allocation strategies, Jim Jones and Barbara Smith suddenly realized that an additional issue needed to be discussed, namely, the potential impact on fund returns of using nontraditional asset classes (that is, classes other than stocks, bonds, and bills) or alternative investment strategies. In particular, because real bonds, although a possible future offering, were not yet issued by the U.S. government, they wondered whether any of the following asset classes or investment strategies could be used in place of real bonds:

- real estate,
- gold,
- diversified international stock and bond portfolios,
- baskets of collateralized commodities, or
- tactical asset allocation, defined as the active management of short-term asset-mix shifts.

Given the availability of these alternate asset classes or investment approaches, how might Smith and Jones alter the asset allocation strategies to be recommended to their respective boards?

A Tale of Two Pension Funds: Case Analysis (A)

In making strategic asset allocation recommendations for their pension funds, Jim Jones and Barbara Smith face a problem shared by every pension fund manager: how to maximize the return on the portfolio for an appropriate level of risk. To find the solutions to this problem, Jones and Smith must keep in mind the pension fund balance sheet (Exhibit 1), which will dictate to a significant degree the risk–return trade-off for each fund.

Both investment managers believe that their investment strategies should be based on a going-concern view of their pension plans. As going concerns, the pension funds must provide for the impact of future wage and inflation experiences on pension fund liabilities. Jones and Smith agree that the immunizing investment strategy would combine some fixed-rate bonds with inflation-indexed bonds and, possibly, a small equity position to hedge against unknown future trends in wages. Deciding the funds' appropriate long-term investment strategies, however, requires addressing two further issues.

First, the U.S. Treasury is not yet issuing inflation-indexed bonds. So, what substitute asset(s) or alternative strategies can be used for an inflation hedge?

Second, how much incremental return should each fund seek relative to the return produced by the immunizing strategies? Any incremental return realized will reduce the contributions required to finance the promised benefits under the plans. Because Alpha Corporation is a private-sector corporation seeking to maximize shareholder wealth and the Public Sector Retirement System (PSRS) is sponsored by a state already committed to funding a previous contribution shortfall, both plans would welcome an investment policy that would reduce their required contributions. Thus, Jones and Smith face the difficult task of improving the investment performance of their pension funds in the real world of uncertain future asset-class returns and uncertain future economic conditions shaping those returns.

Developing asset allocation recommendations that will earn a return beyond the ideal immunizing strategy requires a forecast of the expected returns for different asset classes under different economic conditions, and a determination of the asset allocation combination that appears to offer the best return opportunities relative to the immunizing strategy. Jones has started this process by developing the forecasts of asset-class returns for 1994 through 1998 given in Table 2 of the A case. To complete the analysis, three questions must be addressed:

- How realistic are Jones's estimates of the returns for the 1994–98 period?
- If the estimates are realistic, what are the estimated returns for different portfolio compositions in the three different economic scenarios for the 1994–98 period?
- What asset allocation strategies should Jones and Smith recommend to their boards of directors or trustees?

The historical returns of different asset classes in different economic conditions (Table 1 of the A case) can be used to evaluate Jones's projected returns. To use this historical information effectively, Smith and Jones need to categorize the different historical periods in line with the definitions for the three projected scenarios—degearing, inflation, or deflation. In terms of economic growth and inflation, the 1952–65 period corresponds most closely to the degearing definition, the 1928–40 period to the deflation definition, and the 1966–81 period to the inflation definition.

Note, however, that the expected

economic conditions for 1994–98 do not closely match *any* of the past periods in Table 1. For example, in the 1952–65 period, the economy was characterized by higher economic growth (3.3 percent GNP growth) and lower inflation (1.4 percent) than is projected for the degearing scenario. The degearing scenario assumes that the U.S. economy will grow slowly during the decade (2.5 percent increase in annual GNP growth) as Federal Reserve tight-money policies hold down the level of inflation (to 3.0 percent annually) and the United States works its way out of a debt overhang and large federal government deficits.

Given its assumptions as to real GNP growth and inflation and the 1994 structure of interest rates and dividend yields, the degearing scenario projects real returns for bills of 1.5 percent, for bonds of 3.25 percent, and for stocks of 5.25 percent. The comparison 1952–65 period experienced real returns for bills of 1.3 percent, for bonds of –0.2 percent, and for stocks of 13.1 percent. Although the actual and projected experiences for bills are similar, the actual and projected experiences for bonds and stocks are very different. The difference lies in the higher economic growth and lower inflation of the 1952–66 period, which drew money into stocks and thus increased stock multiples and improved stock returns; at the same time, bond yields were low in the early 1950s and rising interest rates worked to depress bond returns. After adjustments are made for these differences, the returns projected in Table 2 for the degearing scenario appear realistic.

Similar differences exist between the projected economic forecasts and asset-class returns for the deflation and the inflation scenarios and their comparable historical periods. Overall, Jones's real-return projections for the period of the late 1990s show bill returns similar to their historical experiences but generally better bond returns and poorer stock returns relative to their historical experiences.

Why would Jones project experiences for the future that appear to be significantly different from the experi-

ences of the past? The answer to this questions lies in his assumption that a stock market correction will occur if, instead of degearing, either a deflation or inflation scenario occurs. Jones apparently assumes that the deflation scenario, particularly if started by a collapse of the Japanese economy, would result in substantially increased fears about the future of the global economy, a lowering of expectations for corporate profits, and increased fears about the outlook for stocks. This outcome would generate an increase in the risk premium on stocks, resulting in negative returns on stocks in the 1994–98 period. In contrast, bond returns would be enhanced as bond prices rose with a drop in long-term interest rates accompanying the switch to a deflation scenario. Jones is apparently suggesting that, in an inflation scenario, higher capitalization-rate requirements would, again, lower the returns to stocks because of stock price declines. Bond prices and returns would suffer even more than stocks in this scenario.

Disagreement with Jones's assumptions regarding the market reaction to the deflation and inflation scenarios and the subsequent impact on stocks would lead to projected returns more attuned to historical averages. His assumption of a market correction appears reasonable, however, in light of the long bull market reflected in the returns to stocks in the 1982–93 period and the market's historically adverse reaction in short periods to *unexpected* deflationary and inflationary environments as the market seeks new equilibrium levels.

Assuming that the projected returns in the different scenarios are reasonable, Smith and Jones can calculate reasonable returns for each of the four alternative portfolios in the three scenarios. The portfolio returns are the weighted averages of the projected asset-class returns for each economic scenario. The weightings would be the percentages each asset class represents in the particular portfolio. The weighted real returns of particular portfolios in the three economic scenarios are given in **Table A**. Cash was given no weighting in any of

Table A. Weighted-Average Real Returns of Selected Portfolios by Economic Scenario

Asset Mix	Degearing	Deflation	Inflation
70% equity/30% debt	4.65%	−4.35%	−2.60%
60% equity/40% debt	4.45	−2.80	−2.80
50% equity/50% debt	4.25	−1.25	−3.00
40% equity/60% debt	4.05	0.30	−3.20

the portfolios suggested for analysis and is not included in any of the portfolio descriptions.

The different portfolios exhibit significantly different return performance in the three economic scenarios. In the degearing scenario, an equity-heavy portfolio performs slightly better than a debt-heavy scenario, but in a deflation scenario, a debt-heavy portfolio performs significantly better than an equity-heavy portfolio. Although none of the portfolio mixes performs well in the inflation scenario, an equity-heavy portfolio does somewhat better than a debt-heavy portfolio.

These return differences have significant implications for the asset-mix recommendations Jones and Smith should make to their boards. If, as Smith apparently believes, a good possibility exists that the degearing scenario could deteriorate into deflation, then the portfolio should be debt heavy. This strategy would not significantly reduce returns in the degearing scenario but would provide significant protection against the downside of deflation. In the inflation scenario, a shading toward equity should produce the best (or least worst) results. If the inflation scenario is a viable possibility, the only hedge available would be a sizable allocation of the portfolio to cash equivalents (T-bills).

Based on the three possible scenarios, which of the four portfolio alternatives evaluated in Table A should be recommended for the Alpha Corporation fund and the PSRS fund?

Alpha Corporation's current asset mix of 70 percent equity/30 percent debt reflects the company's ability and willingness to assume larger risk than the PSRS. If the asset-mix strategy does not produce the desired real-return results, Jones would have to inform the board of directors that a larger future contribution to the corporation's pension plan is required to provide its future defined benefits. The result would be a reduction of corporate cash available for other purposes for a time. In conclusion, given the possible capital market environments for 1994 through 1998, and given Jones's view that inflation is more likely than deflation, Alpha Corporation is likely to maintain its 70 percent equity/30 percent debt strategy.

The PSRS's current asset mix of 50 percent equity/50 percent debt reflects its concerns about unfunded future liabilities and its resulting greater risk aversion (relative to Alpha Corporation). If the PSRS's strategy does not produce the desired real returns, the system must request funds from the state government, which involves raising taxes or cutting expenditures, and from the employees, which involves additional contributions from their salaries. Neither necessity would be painless. Therefore, given the possible 1994–98 environments and given Smith's view that deflation is more likely than inflation, the PSRS might find a 10-percentage-point shift from equity to debt desirable. The resulting mix, 40 percent equity/60 percent debt, would be relatively conservative. In addition, because of the inflation sensitivity of the plan's liabilities, the PSRS should consider shortening the duration of the debt portfolio.

A Tale of Two Pension Funds: Case Analysis (B)

Whereas the analysis in the A case calculated weighted returns for different asset mixes in which only two asset classes were considered, the B case presents the same analysis with calculations for three asset classes under the assumptions of the three economic scenarios. As in the A case, the real returns for equities and fixed-rate bonds are taken from Table 2 of the A case; the real returns for real bonds are given in the last paragraph of the B case. Using these returns to calculate the weighted-average returns for the portfolios including the real debt produces the expected real portfolio returns given in **Table B**. As in the A case, cash was given no weight in any of the portfolios and is not included in the portfolio descriptions.

The computation of returns for the five portfolios in Table B for the three economic scenarios results in significantly different portfolio performance. In addition, the inclusion of real bonds has significantly different impacts on the portfolios in the different scenarios. Under the terms of the degearing scenario, real bonds significantly erode portfolio performance, and the greater the percentage of real bonds, the more sharply performance erodes. In both the deflation and inflation scenarios, however, real bonds substantially improve performance; performance improves steadily as the percentage of real bonds increases.

The impact of real bonds on portfolio performance is significant and should be reflected in the asset-mix recommendations of Jim Jones and Barbara Smith. Specifically, the two managers should recommend the inclusion of real bonds in their portfolios to the extent that the managers wish to reduce the exposure of their portfolios to the risks associated with deflation and inflation. The greater the likelihood a manager

attaches to inflation or deflation, the greater the emphasis he or she should place on real bonds in the asset mix.

The liabilities of both pension plans are sensitive to inflation, although those of the PSRS are the more sensitive. For example, when inflation occurs, the Alpha Corporation is expected to *consider* increasing pension benefits, but inflation-caused benefit increases at Alpha are purely ad hoc or discretionary. The PSRS has a more formal mechanism for systematically matching pension benefit increases to inflation increases.

Because of the poor performance expected of the first three asset mixes in Table B in the inflation scenario, none of those three mixes should be recommended if the inflation scenario has a large chance of occurrence. The fourth mix, 0 percent equity/40 percent fixed debt/60 percent real debt, is the mix that should immunize the typical North American (private-sector) corporation pension plan's liabilities. That is, it will produce the scenario returns needed to stabilize the pension plan balance sheet.[1] The fifth asset mix, 0 percent equity/20 percent fixed debt/80 percent real debt, is the immunizing portfolio for the typical public-sector pension plan that is formally and systematically indexed to price inflation, such as the PSRS plan. Such plans need more inflation tracking to match pension liabilities than do private-sector plans.

To summarize, Jones and the Alpha Corporation will want to reduce the pension fund's exposure to equities, increase the use of real bonds, and at the same time, take an amount of risk that reflects the corporation's ability to make pension fund contributions should a

---

[1]Immunizing balance-sheet risk involves matching asset volatility to liability volatility. Thus, although assets in a pension fund may have substantial volatility, if the balance sheet is immunized, that volatility will be essentially 100 percent positively correlated with pension liability.

Table B. Weighted-Average Returns for Portfolios Including Equity, Fixed-Rate Debt, and Real Debt by Scenario

Asset Mix	Degearing	Deflation	Inflation
70% equity/30% fixed debt/0% real debt	4.65%	−4.35%	−2.60%
50% equity/50% fixed debt/0% real debt	4.25	−1.25	−3.00
40% equity/40% fixed debt/20% real debt	3.90	−1.00	−1.66
0% equity/40% fixed debt/60% real debt	2.80	2.60	0.62
0% equity/20% fixed debt/80% real debt	2.65	1.30	2.16

worst-case scenario (e.g., inflation) occur. Thus, Alpha's mix might be changed from 70 percent equity/30 percent fixed debt to 60 percent equity/30 percent fixed debt/10 percent real debt.

Smith and the PSRS will want to reduce exposure to equities even more than Alpha because of the PSRS's higher sensitivity to inflation and greater aversion to balance-sheet risk. Smith and the PSRS have a greater need than the Alpha Corporation to avoid unfavorable real-return outcomes in any of the three possible scenarios. As a result, Smith should recommend a shift from the current 50 percent equity/50 percent fixed debt asset mix to a mix of 40 percent equity/20 percent fixed debt/40 percent real debt. As with the revised mix for Alpha, this mix should reduce variability of real returns for the PSRS in all three possible scenarios but be more aggressive (have more balance-sheet risk exposure) than the typical public fund's immunizing portfolio.

The arguments for Jones and Smith to use real bonds in their funds' asset-mix strategies depend on the managers' expectations of the likelihood of the deflation or inflation scenarios. The recommended revisions assume that each of the three economic scenarios has a reasonable chance of occurring. That is, even though one scenario, degearing, appears to be the best characterization of what the economy and the capital markets will do, the other two scenarios could realistically occur, and investment strategy must recognize that fact.

A Tale of Two Pension Funds: Case Analysis (C)

The asset classes and strategies introduced in this case would probably be used to moderate the downside risk associated with the principal asset classes of equities and bonds. One economic scenario with significant downside risk for both equities and bonds is the inflation scenario. Real bonds are intended to reduce the downside risk in this scenario, but as the C case explains, real bonds were not available in the United States at the time of case series. Therefore, Jim Jones and Barbara Smith must consider alternative asset classes (such as real estate, gold, international securities, and collateralized commodities) or investment strategies (such as tactical asset allocation) with return attributes potentially similar to those of real bonds.

To determine how the additional asset classes/strategies might carry out the purpose of reducing downside risk requires assessing how the asset classes would perform in the different economic scenarios. For example, making the calculations for a diversified portfolio of commercial real estate in a degearing scenario produces the following: If the portfolio were to have a real return in the 1994–98 period of 3.5 percent (an unlevered cash-on-cash yield of 9.5 percent equal to 6.5 percent net of depreciation, which is then reduced by the degearing inflation rate of 3.0 percent), then that portfolio might be considered an acceptable substitute for real bonds. Using a similar approach to calculate real returns in the deflation and inflation scenarios results in real returns for real estate of –1.0 percent under deflation and 5.5 percent under inflation. Because real bonds had hypothetical real returns of 2.5 percent, 0.0 percent, and 3.7 percent in the degearing, deflation, and inflation scenarios, respectively, real estate appears to be a reasonable alternative to real bonds.

The historical record suggests that gold is a reliable inflation hedge. How gold would behave in deflation is not clear; the price would be expected to drop, but if a global banking crisis was associated with deflation, people would seek gold (in hard form, not as gold stocks) as a hedge against economic chaos. In the degearing scenario, gold would not be likely to produce any real return because slow, stable economic growth would reduce the desirability of holding gold and price changes would likely be nil. For purposes of portfolio analysis, gold could be assumed to produce a 6.0 percent real return in the inflation scenario (somewhat better than real estate because of better liquidity), a –9.0 percent real return (similar to equities) in the deflation scenario, and a 0.0 percent real return in degearing.

The extent to which a portfolio of diversified international stocks and bonds would hedge the funds against deflationary or inflationary forces in the United States would depend on how globally synchronized the forces and their effects on security prices were. For purposes of portfolio analysis, the effects of the forces can be assumed to be less outside the United States than inside and the differences in returns on diversified international stocks and bonds can be assumed to be less extreme across the scenarios than the returns on U.S. stocks and bonds. Estimating these returns requires subjective judgments because the case does not provide detailed data about a potential international portfolio. The analyst must balance three elements to reach an estimate of real returns: the (unknown) extent to which the international economy is following the economic trend in the United States, the (unknown) mix of stocks and bonds in the international portfolio, and the (unknown) projected real returns on international stocks and bonds.

In the absence of case information

on the "unknowns," the following general assumptions can be made to develop subjective estimates of the three elements. First, the international economy would be following the U.S. trend but would not be as pronounced; that is, the international economy would be experiencing less degearing, less deflation, or less inflation. Second, the mix between stocks and bonds would be 60 percent equity/40 percent debt. Third, the real returns on international stocks and bonds would be similar to U.S. returns in the same economic scenarios. Based on these assumptions, reasonable estimates of real returns for the international portfolio would be 4.0 percent in degearing, –4.0 percent in deflation, and 0.0 percent in inflation. Note that these subjective estimates are point estimates; a more complete analysis would calculate the impact of substitution based on the entire distribution of potential returns.

Another potential asset class, collateralized commodities, would probably fall between the performance of real estate and gold in terms of return behavior. More research would be required, however, for Smith and Jones to establish the detailed characteristics of this asset class.

The various effects of substituting the alternatives to real bonds can be seen by computing the returns of selected portfolios using the real-bond substitutes. For instance, **Table C** gives the returns calculated for adding various real-debt substitutes to two asset-mix strategies from the B case, a 40 percent fixed-rate debt/60 percent real debt strategy and a 20 percent fixed-rate debt/80 percent real debt strategy.

Table C indicates that, in performance terms, real estate would be a good substitute for real bonds, international diversification would be partly satisfactory, and gold would be a poor substitute. The implication is that Jones and Smith should recommend the use of real estate in their overall strategy in the same proportions they would recommend real bonds. If the illiquidity of real estate is an issue, then the two managers should include a diversified portfolio of international stocks and bonds in their recommendations.

Tactical asset allocation, defined as the active management of short-term asset-mix shifts, should be viewed as an alternative investment strategy, not as an asset-class substitute for real bonds. Tactical asset allocation offers good hedging potential if the fund managers can anticipate major upward or downward movements of stock and bond prices and can buy or sell, as appropriate, before these major shifts occur. In a situation of perfect tactical asset allocation, in which the portfolio manager could forecast future economic scenarios with 100 percent accuracy and quickly adjust the portfolio asset mix accordingly, the portfolio manager would, indeed, never lose money, because the concentration of the portfolio would always be moved to those asset classes with the most positive returns. In such an ideal situation, returns to tactical asset allocation could be assumed to be the best available for any asset class

Table C. Weighted-Average Returns by Scenario for Selected Portfolios Using Alternative Asset Classes or Strategies

Asset-Mix Strategy	Degearing	Deflation	Inflation
40% fixed debt/60% real debt	2.80%	2.60%	0.62%
40% fixed debt/60% real estate	3.40	2.00	1.70
40% fixed debt/60% gold	1.30	–2.80	2.00
40% fixed debt/60% diversified international	3.70	0.20	–1.60
20% fixed debt/80% real debt	2.65	1.30	2.16
20% fixed debt/80% real estate	4.10	0.50	3.60
20% fixed debt/80% gold	0.65	–5.90	4.00
20% fixed debt/80% diversified international	3.85	–1.90	-1.20

in that economic scenario.

In the real world, however, achieving the returns associated with perfect asset allocation is impossible for several reasons. The first is the difficulty of forecasting with certainty what capital markets will actually do. The second reason is the practical problems associated with moving large blocks of investment capital in major pension funds between different asset classes in short periods of time. The third reason is the restrictions on investment policies typically imposed on pension funds by internal investment guidelines and by legal requirements. These restrictions alone, particularly legal requirements relating to asset mix, are enough to make perfect tactical asset allocation impossible.

Some use of tactical asset allocation should be considered, however, if processes can be identified that have better than a 50 percent chance of success. For purposes of portfolio analysis, successful tactical asset allocation can be assumed to add a modest return increment (i.e., 50–100 basis points) to the strategic asset-mix return in the deflation and inflation scenarios.

Order Form ₀₈₆

Additional copies of *Investment Policy* (and other AIMR publications listed on page 85) are available for purchase. Simply complete this form and return it via mail or fax to:

PBD, Inc.
P.O. Box 6996
Alpharetta, Ga. 30239-6996
U.S.A.
Telephone: 800/789-AIMR • Fax: 404/442-9742

Name _____

Company_____

Address _____

_____Suite/Floor _____

City_____

State _____ ZIP _____Country _____

Daytime Telephone _____Fax _____

Title of Publication	Price	Qty.	Total
_____	_____	_____	_____
_____	_____	_____	_____

SHIPPING/HANDLING CHARGES: Included in price of book for all U.S. orders. Surface delivery to Canada and Mexico, add $12 if value of books purchased is less than $50, or 18% of the total if value is between $50 and $100. Priority (air) delivery to Canada and Mexico, add $25 if value of books is less than $50, or 33% of the total if value is between $50 and $100. Other international purchasers should call or fax PBD for a shipping quote. **DISCOUNTS:** Students, professors, and university libraries, 25%; CFA candidates (ID #_____), 25%; retired members (ID #_____), 25%; 50 or more copies of the same title, 40%.	Discount $ —_____ 4.5% sales tax (Virginia residents) $ _____ 8.25% sales tax (New York residents) $ _____ 7% GST (Canada residents, #124134602) $ _____ 6% sales tax (Georgia residents) $ _____ Shipping/handling $ _____ **Total cost of order** $ _____

☐ Check or money order enclosed payable to **PBD, Inc.**
Charge to: ☐ VISA   ☐ Mastercard   ☐ American Express   ☐ Discover

Card Number: ☐☐☐☐☐☐☐☐☐☐☐☐☐☐☐☐

Signature:_____   Expiration date: _____

Selected AIMR Publications*

Investing Worldwide V, 1994 . . . . $30

**Analysts' Earnings Forecast Accuracy in Japan and the
United States**, 1994 . . . . $20
Robert M. Conroy, Robert S. Harris, and Young S. Park

The Automotive Industry, 1994 . . . . $30
Theodore Shasta, CFA, *Editor*

The Telecommunications Industry, 1994 . . . . $30
Randall S. Billingsley, CFA, *Editor*

Managed Futures and Their Role in Investment Portfolios, 1994 . . . $30
Don M. Chance, CFA

Fundamentals of Cross-Border Investment: The European View,
1994 . . . . $20
Bruno Solnik

Good Ethics: The Essential Element of a Firm's Success, 1994 . . . . $30
H. Kent Baker, CFA, *Editor*

A Practitioner's Guide to Factor Models, 1994 . . . . $30

Quality Management and Institutional Investing, 1994 . . . . $30
Keith P. Ambachtsheer, *Editor*

Managing Emerging Market Portfolios, 1994 . . . . $30
John W. Peavy III, CFA, *Editor*

Global Asset Management and Performance Attribution, 1994 . . . . $30
Denis S. Karnosky, Ph.D., and Brian D. Singer, CFA

Franchise Value and the Price/Earnings Ratio, 1994 . . . . $30
Martin L. Leibowitz and Stanley Kogelman

Investing Worldwide, 1993, 1992, 1991, 1990 . . . . $30 each

The Modern Role of Bond Covenants, 1994 . . . . $20
Ileen B. Malitz

Derivative Strategies for Managing Portfolio Risk, 1993 . . . . $30
Keith C. Brown, CFA, *Editor*

Equity Securities Analysis and Evaluation, 1993 . . . . $30

**The CAPM Controversy: Policy and Strategy Implications for
Investment Management**, 1993 . . . . $30
Diana R. Harrington and Robert A. Korajczyk, *Editors*

The Health Care Industry, 1993 . . . . $30
James Balog, *Editor*

**Predictable Time-Varying Components of International
Asset Returns**, 1993 . . . . $20
Bruno Solnik

---

*A full catalog of publications is available from AIMR, P.O. Box 3668, Charlottesville, Va.
22903; 804/980-9712; fax 804/980-3634.